Moving Beyond Belief

Moving Beyond Belief

A Strategy for Personal Growth

THOMAS NELSON PUBLISHERS

Nashville

Published in Nashville, Tennessee, by Thomas Nelson, Inc.

Unless otherwise noted, Scripture quotations are from the NEW KING JAMES VERSION of the Bible. Copyright © 1979, 1980, 1982, Thomas Nelson, Inc., Publishers.

The Gathering/USA, Inc. is an evangelical, nonprofit organization with a mission to mobilize and participate with the church to evangelize and disciple men and women. This is accomplished through sponsoring city-wide outreach breakfasts or lunch gatherings, Bible study groups and individual discipleship. For more information about our organization, please contact:

The Gathering/USA, Inc.
106 East Church Street
Orlando, FL 32801
(407) 422-9200
FAX: (407) 839-4023

Printed in the United States of America

2 3 4 5 6 — 98 97 96 95 94 93

DEDICATION

This book is dedicated to the memory and ongoing ministry of Jim Smith, formerly the Associate Pastor of Highland Park Presbyterian Church in Dallas, Texas.

Jim not only taught about a personal and progressive commitment to Christ, he lived it. His final progression was into the arms of Christ early in 1993 after a battle with cancer. All who were led to faith, restored through his teaching, or renewed through his counseling, are grateful for the new insights and "ah ha's" that he opened to us.

ACKNOWLEDGMENT

We are grateful for the authors who each contributed a chapter to this book. They did so desiring to give the many men who are coming to Christ through The Gathering a foundational study for their new faith.

CONTENTS

Personal and Progressive Commitment in Your Relationship to the Body of Christ

Personal and Progressive Commitment to the Work of Christ in the World

FOREWORD

I have had the privilege of speaking for numerous Gathering of Men events across the country over the past several years. Although my schedule has been packed with the demands of managing an NBA franchise, I find time for The Gathering because of the impact I have observed firsthand.

Seeing scores of men come to a personal faith in Christ and other men assume spiritual leadership in their communities has been very rewarding. These men are moving beyond the elementary understanding of their belief. Now they have the opportunity for a study that will facilitate their continuing personal growth.

This new book comes at just the right time. Go through it yourself. Take another man through it with you. Form a small study group or teach it in a larger setting. You will find the experience rewarding.

> — Pat Williams
> General Manager and President
> Orlando Magic NBA Basketball Team

INTRODUCTION

The years 1974-78 were a pivotal time in my spiritual and career development. I was on staff at Highland Park Presbyterian Church in Dallas, working with high school students. I enjoyed my relationships with the other church staff members. We had a strong sense of community, and the work with students was challenging and going well. However, that was also a time when seeds were being planted for a new ministry that eventually would develop into a national outreach to men.

I had a heart for men and enjoyed spending time with a small group that met weekly. We studied the Scriptures, challenged each other to grow spiritually, and shared the struggles that all men experience. We called ourselves the Bible Buddies.

One of the men in the group was John Kidd, a Dallas attorney. John is very bright and has a voracious appetite for the Scriptures. He consumed everything he could get his hands on relating to the Christian life. He also made a lot of money developing real estate in the Metroplex. During those years, the Texas economy was booming, and everyone thought there would be no end to the fortunes being made in oil and land.

But all of that changed dramatically in the late 1980s. As the economy decompressed, business opportunities slowed to a trickle. Since this negative economic environment stymied real estate, John concentrated on discipling other men—full-time. Today he studies the Bible with them and encourages them to grow in the same ways I had challenged him over a decade before. He is a classic example of a man who has moved beyond a one-dimensional belief.

Belief certainly has an intellectual side, for an accumulation of facts must always form the basis for determining truth. Therefore, if Christianity is to have substance, it has to be built on reputable scholarship, reputable history, and intellectual discernment. But true biblical belief goes much further. It demands a commitment to live as Christ wants you to live. This definition is inherent in the word "disciple". A disciple is one who learns the ways of Christ and follows in His steps.

This manual places strong emphasis on what it means to be the kind of believer who is changed by what he learns and in turn changes his world. The concept is based on something Howard Hendricks said: "True learning only takes place when it alters your behavior."

The best way I know to determine whether behavior is being altered is to look at a man's schedule. You show me your Daytimer or your calendar, and I'll tell you the priorities you live by. Show it to me again in six months, and we'll both know if you've changed your priorities.

Exposure to truth doesn't mean a man will allow the truth to transform him. Transforming truth involves change, and there's nothing a man resists more than change. But if we want to develop spiritually, change is absolutely crucial.

For the past twenty years I have attempted by God's grace to allow transforming truth to shape my life. I pray that this manual will be the launching pad for the same kind of commitment in your life.

— John Tolson
Chairman of the Board
The Gathering/USA, Inc.

CHAPTER 1

PERSONAL AND PROGRESSIVE COMMITMENT TO JESUS CHRIST

Jim Smith
Highland Park Presbyterian Church, Dallas, Texas

■ CHAPTER OBJECTIVE ■

"What does commitment to Christ mean?"
"How does a person grown in the faith?" "How does my mind relate to this process?" In this chapter, you will learn how to grow and mature in the Christian faith.

THE BEGINNING

Your relationship with Christ began when you prayed and gave your life to Him. But that was just the beginning. Think of a marriage. A wedding anniversary commemorates when a man and woman pledge their lives to each other. But that wedding ceremony, that public commitment, is just the beginning of life together. From that day on, their relationship grows, develops and matures.

Or consider a newborn baby. When he enters the world, cold and hungry, he is born into a new life, and yearly birthday celebrations commemorate that important date. But the birth day also is just a beginning; he grows and develops daily.

And that's what should happen in your new Christian life. You have been born spiritually—like the newborn baby. Now you have to begin to grow.

GROWING IN CHRIST

Growing in the Christian faith involves a personal and progressive commitment. It is personal because it involves you. It is progressive because it is dynamic, continuing to grow and change as you do.

It is a commitment (like when you accepted Christ as your Savior) because it involves giving yourself.

Here's an explanation I hope you'll remember: Personal and progressive commitment means that you daily give all you understand about yourself to God, which results in letting God work through your life for the benefit of others.

SELF-AWARENESS

Two dynamics affect how we understand commitment and the degree of our commitment. Obviously one of them is self-awareness—what we understand about ourselves. Growth, then, involves continually improving our self-awareness—understanding why we do the things we do. Since what a person believes as a child may affect who he is as an adult, self-awareness would include understanding one's family—how one was raised, how one grew up.

We are the result of genetics, socialization, spiritual training, and many other factors. All of these things have an impact on who we are as adults. The better we understand that, the better the chance we have of understanding the difference between being driven as a Christian and being called as one. In other words, the more we learn about ourselves, the more we can give ourselves to God, and the more He can work in and through us.

The first step of personal growth, then, is self-awareness.

GOD-AWARENESS

The second step is God-awareness. As our concept of God changes or matures, so should our commitment to Him. Unfortunately, many misconceptions about God alter or qualify how safe we feel about trusting Him with our lives.

> *The first misconception is the idea that God is a sort of heavenly janitor who sweeps up after you make a mess.*

The first misconception is the idea that God is a sort of heavenly janitor who sweeps up after you make a mess. If this is what you think, then you will only get serious about God when you are in trouble. You believe that God is only there to help you when you really blow it. Or that He's running around with a whisk broom, dust pan, and maybe a little heavenly Elmer's Glue. He cleans up, mops up, and glues us back together, so that we can go out and get in trouble all over again.

Obviously this view of God doesn't call us to a serious commitment. I'm not sure I would want to commit myself to a heavenly custodian.

If you swing the pendulum to the other side, you may think of God as a super Santa Claus who waits for you to page Him on His beeper service. When you page Him, He snaps to, salutes, and carries out your command. This concept defines God as a genie in a bottle. If you believe this, you're going to be disappointed, because God doesn't always act in the way we think He should.

During the Civil War, Abraham Lincoln was asked if he thought God was on his side. With his usual wisdom, Lincoln answered that his greatest concern was whether or not he was on God's side. Lincoln demonstrated a mature understanding of God.

Of course we in the church perpetuate this misconception to some degree by emphasizing answered prayer, casting all of our cares upon God, and taking all of our needs to Him. Those concepts are true and right; but if you think of God as a genie who waits for your command, you're in trouble. A servant won't demand anything of you or push you to achieve your potential.

A third misconception is that God is impersonal, far removed from us, and that He doesn't care. Some people believe that God is emotionally and personally removed from His creation. They may think this because they can't understand Him—He seems so distant and unknowable. Or perhaps they see the evil and suffering in the world and can't reconcile it with a loving God.

I realize there is no way we can totally understand God. Instead, we catch glimpses of Him. We're like blind men trying to describe an elephant by only touching his tail. But to see God as cold, aloof, and uncaring contradicts everything Jesus taught. Jesus said that God was a loving father.

If you believe that God is distant and unconcerned about the world, you won't be drawn to Him or want to give Him your life.

> *We're like blind men trying to describe an elephant by only touching his tail.*

Another misconception is that God wears a denominational label. He is either Baptist or Methodist or Assembly of God or Catholic or you name it. People who believe this carry God around in a box. Whenever they get near someone from a different religious background, whose idea or understanding of God doesn't fit in their box, they lock the lid and refuse to listen.

When we try to contain God within some kind of creed or formalized theology, we run the risk of reducing Him to a safe pattern we can deal with, but one that doesn't describe Him at all.

As we mature and grow in our God-realization, we must balance two truths, both of which are taught in Scripture. The first truth is that God is the astounding Creator of the universe. This goes beyond the human mind's ability to comprehend. David expressed it well in Psalm 8:3-4: "When I consider Your heavens, the work of

Your fingers, the moon and the stars, which You have ordained, What is man that You are mindful of him, And the son of man that You visit him?"

The second truth is that we finite beings find our connection to the infinite God through Christ. This personal relationship is described in the Bible in the most intimate of family terms as a father-son relationship.

In the Lord's prayer, Christ taught us to address God as Father (Matt. 6:6-15). Elsewhere He taught that we could call God "Abba, Father," similar to calling Him Daddy (Mark 14:36; Rom. 8:15).

So we wrestle with the tension that God is our creator, sovereign, and ruler of the universe—all the terms that theologians use—yet He is our friend, our father, and the lover of our souls.

PERSONAL COMMITMENT

We've discussed self-awareness and we've looked at God-awareness. Now let's consider what is meant by "personal commitment."

First of all, commitment by its very definition is personal. It involves our total being—our intellect and our emotions.

If we have feeling without intellect, we're in trouble. If we have intellect without feeling, we're superficial. Our commitment to Christ involves both.

We can only commit ourselves, not anyone else. As much as we would like to commit our wives, or husbands, children, and friends, they must come to Christ on their own. We can encourage them, but we can't believe for them. That's why it is called personal commitment.

PROGRESSIVE COMMITMENT

Finally we come to "progressive commitment." As I mentioned at the beginning of the chapter, Christian growth is dynamic, a daily process of giving ourselves to God.

In other words, as we become progressively aware of ourselves, through Bible study, prayer, counseling, and life's circumstances, we must continue to commit that new information, those growth areas, to Christ.

Self-awareness is complex because people are complex. None of us is as simple as we seem. The more accurately we know who we are, the more we will be able to grow in faith.

As a therapist and a counselor, I spend a great deal of time helping people better understand who they are, why they do what they do, and what areas of their lives may need God's healing and wholeness. When they understand these things, they are no longer driven or compulsive, nor do they exhibit personality behaviors and disorders.

Unfortunately, some people think that just because a person is a Christian, he or she won't have any problems, especially emotional problems. Following Christ won't necessarily solve a neurosis.

Self-awareness, then, will reveal areas of your life that you can ask God to heal. If you are consumed by hatred or bitterness, if you were abused as a child, or something else happened that has radically affected who you are as an adult, you can be healed as you allow God to enter your life.

> . . . *following Christ won't necessarily solve a neurosis.*

We were all reared by less than perfect parents, and the sins of the fathers do get passed on to second, third, and fourth generations. As we learn about ourselves, we give those areas to God. That's called progressive commitment.

PUTTING IT TOGETHER

Now that we understand our terms, here's the process. First of all, there is a starting point when a person decides if he is going to commit himself to God or to something else. There comes a time when you say, "I'm not going to make it if I keep trying to run the show by myself." And by faith you commit yourself to Christ.

This means that you're under new management. Then, day by day, you commit each new awareness of yourself to God.

There's a very real sense in which we get up every morning and have some new awareness of who we are and why we do what we do, or we have a new awareness of our own woundedness. We then turn that over to God.

We all operate below the conscious level, doing certain things without knowing why we do them. But as we become aware of these forces, tendencies, and desires, we can confess them and say: "Lord, I don't want to do that any more. I don't want to behave that way. I don't want to react or respond that way anymore." Then we can ask God to bring healing or give us courage to change.

> *Any person who is growing has new awareness, new insights, new "Ah ha's!" daily.*

The Christian life is an adventure of watching God's work in our lives. He changes and shapes us into the kind of people He wants us to be. It's an exciting life of personal, progressive commitment to the Lord of the universe.

As you read this book, you will learn much about yourself, your relationships with others, and your relationship with God. Keep reading, keep learning, and keep giving all you know of yourself to all you know of God.

■ GROWTH STRATEGIES ■

1. What do these passages teach about Christian growth?

   Mark 9:23-24

   Luke 9:23-25

   Romans 14:20-23

   1 Corinthians 3:1-3

   Philippians 1:6

   Colossians 3:1-4

   Hebrews 5:12-14

2. What was your understanding of God five years ago? What were your goals in life?

3. How has your understanding of God changed? What are your goals now?

4. Since becoming a Christian, how has your life changed in these areas:

   prayer

   concern for others

   family

   worship

5. What will you do over the next five years to learn more about God?

6. What can you do in the near future to grow in your relationship with Christ?

Personal and Progressive Commitment in Your Relationship with God

CHAPTER 2

ASSURANCE OF SALVATION

Harvey Hook
Executive Director,
The Gathering / Columbus

■ CHAPTER OBJECTIVE ■

Let's take a look at some of the questions you may be asking. If you've just recently asked the Lord to come into your life and take control of it, you may be thinking, "I'm a rational being, intelligent, practical, competent, and self-reliant. Why, then, did I just enter into a personal relationship with the Creator of the universe? What does all this mean?"

AM I ONE OF THOSE "SAVED" PEOPLE?

Salvation is a broad and comprehensive term referring to God's plan to restore you to a right relationship with Him. You were "saved" from sin and "saved" to eternal life. In addition, you will be progressively freed from your self-centeredness and brought into harmony with your fellow man. At this point you have acknowledged your sin and need of forgiveness (Rom. 3:23; 6:23); believed that Jesus Christ died on the cross to pay the price for your sins (John 3:16; 1 Peter 3:18); and confessed Christ as your personal Lord and Savior (Eph. 2:8–9; John 1:12–13).

HAVE ALL CHRISTIANS HAD THIS SAME EXPERIENCE?

There are many people today who call themselves Christians who have never been born into the family of God. John 3 tells the story of a religious leader named Nicodemus who kept all the laws and obeyed all the practices of his religious faith. Jesus said to him, "Most assuredly, I say to you, unless one is born again, he cannot see the Kingdom of God" (v. 3). The true believer in Christ has been born twice: first, by a physical birth into a natural family; and second, by a spiritual birth into God's family.

Now that you have truly believed in Christ, you are a child of God: "But as many as received Him, to them He gave the right to become children of God, even to those who believe in His name: who were born, not of blood, nor of the will of the flesh, nor of the will of man, but of God" (John 1:12-13). In light of this, we understand that only the person who has accepted Christ can truly be called a Christian or child of God.

AM I SUPPOSED TO FEEL DIFFERENTLY?

Faith in God does not necessarily mean you will or should feel differently. Faith in Christ is first and foremost a belief that Christ is the Son of God and that He will do what He said He would. When you asked Him to come into your life you exercised your will to commit yourself to Him, and asked Him to become the leader of your life. Faith is not an emotional reaction. It involves your intellect and will. "Now faith is the substance of things hoped for, the evidence of things not seen" (Heb. 11:1).

> *Faith in God does not necessarily mean you will or should feel differently. Faith in Christ is first and foremost a belief that Christ is the Son of God and that He will do what He said He would. Faith is not an emotional reaction. It involves your intellect and will.*

ISN'T LIVING A GOOD LIFE ENOUGH?

Gandhi lived a moral life, and yet even he was not good enough to get into heaven on that record alone. Mark 12:30-31 records Jesus' definition of the only "good life" capable of gaining entry into heaven—"And you shall love the Lord your God with all your heart, and with all your soul, with all your mind, and with all your strength. . . . 'Love your neighbor as yourself'." No one, apart from Jesus, has ever done this.

First Peter 1:16 says, "Be holy, for I am holy."

In Matthew 19:16-21 we read about a wealthy and well-respected businessman who had gained money, possessions, and prestige in a thoroughly honorable manner. He came to Jesus and asked, "What good thing shall I do that I may have eternal life?"

Without a doubt Jesus' answer surprised this man. "Why do you call me good? No one is good but one, *that is*, God." Jesus was challenging this man's definition of goodness. Only God is good, only that which is born of God and His eternal love is of true, eternal value. Jesus continued, "Keep the commandments . . . 'You shall not murder,' 'You shall not commit adultery,' 'You shall not steal,' 'You shall not bear false witness,' 'Honor your father and your mother' and, 'You shall love your neighbor as yourself.' "

With a sigh of relief, this prosperous young man replied, "All these I have kept from my youth. What do I still lack?"

Jesus responded, "If you want to be perfect, go, sell what you have and give to the poor . . . and come, follow Me." The young man, "went away sorrowful, for he had great possessions." He wanted eternal life but he did not want to depend on the free grace of God alone. Instead, he wanted to work his way there. Perfect goodness is not an external or measurable standard of behavior. It is a measure of our heart's attitude toward God.

> *If it were possible to simply live a good life, Jesus would not have died on the cross for our sins.*

If it were possible to simply live a good life, Jesus would not have died on the cross for our sins. We cannot work our way to God. Salvation is a gift of grace through Jesus Christ (Eph. 1:8-9).

WHAT ELSE DID JESUS SAY AND DO?

Jesus Christ was God incarnate (God in the flesh). He claimed to be God, "I and My Father are one" (John 10:30). Our Christian faith owes its very life and nature to Christ. Mohammed claimed only to be a prophet, and Buddha never claimed to be anything but a man. The same is true for Moses and Confucius. Jesus Christ was fully God and fully man (Titus 2:13; 1 John 5:20).

Jesus Christ lived a fully human life, yet He was free of sin in thought, word, and deed (1 John 3:5). His perfect life qualified Him to be the sacrificial offering for our sins. He took our place and paid our personal debt of sin. We were declared guilty, but Christ took our punishment and declared us "not guilty" if we would receive His free gift of love and undeserved favor—" . . . by one Man's obedience many will be made righteous" (Rom. 5:19).

Jesus Christ died, but He also rose from the dead. The death and resurrection of Christ showed His unique distinction from all other religious leaders of the world: "This Jesus God has raised up, of which we are all witnesses" (Acts 2:32). Because He returned to life, we know we are not placing our faith and trust in a myth. Our sins are completely forgiven. Because He returned to life, we know that we too shall be resurrected to eternal life: "Because I live, you will live also" (John 14:19).

"But," you ask, "how does all this knowledge relate to my day-to-day life in a tough and practical world?"

It forms the very basis of how you approach life! The same power that raised Christ from the grave lives within you through the Holy Spirit. You have His life, His power, and His salvation.

All of this communicates God's love to us: "By this we know love, because He laid down His life for us (1 John 3:16). God chose to become involved in this world of pain and hardship. He sent His Son as a concrete expression of His love for us. We now know that God is not indifferent. He came and walked among us and now lives in the life of every believer.

WHAT CAN I COUNT ON FROM GOD?

You Are Set Free

You have deliverance from the penalty and consequence of sin (John 3:16). While your sins once kept you apart from God, now you have been restored to a right relationship with Him (Eph. 1:7). Because of Christ's death, you have been freed from the penalty of sin and from an eternity of separation from God.

You Have Forgiveness

God has completely forgiven you. "And you, being dead in your trespasses . . . , He has made alive together with Him, having forgiven you all trespasses (Col. 2:13-14). Satan's goal is to destroy your new relationship with God. But when you fail or fall, all you have to do is respond to the mercy of God and confess your faults: "If we confess our sins, He is faithful and just to forgive us our sins and to cleanse us from all unrighteousness" (1 John 1:9).

Christ Is in Your Life

God assures you that His Son Christ has come into your life. In John 14:20 Jesus says, " . . . I am in My Father, and you in Me, and I in you." Christ will remain in your life, He will never leave you. Phil. 1:6 says, " . . . He who has begun a good work in you will complete it until the day of Christ Jesus." His work in you will not be done until He comes to take you home with Him.

God Has Given You the Holy Spirit

God has provided His Holy Spirit to live in you and help you to live the Christian life. The Holy Spirit is God's promise to keep you as one of His own children until Jesus comes for you: "Having believed, you are sealed with the Holy Spirit of promise, who is the guarantee of our inheritance" (Eph. 1:13-14). You can relax; God will speak to you and guide you through His Holy Spirit who now dwells within you.

You Have Eternal Life

God guarantees that you will live forever after your physical life and death: "These things I have written to you who believe in the name of the Son of God, that you may know that you have eternal life" (1 John 5:13). You don't have to guess about this great gift. It's yours, and it's certain. You are simply taking God at His word, and He will never fail you.

You Can Have Victory over Temptation

God's power will provide you with the faith and character to withstand the assaults of this world. You will be tempted, but you can draw confidence from 1 Cor. 10:13: "No temptation has overtaken you except such as is common to man; but God is faithful, who will not allow you to be tempted beyond what you are able, but with the temptation will also make the way of escape, that you may be able to bear it." If you take the temptation to God immediately, He will meet you in your weakness. Temptation is not sin, but it is an indication for you to turn to God in prayer and ask for His assistance.

Jesus Is Coming Again

Jesus has promised to return to earth and gather to heaven all those who believe in Him. Acts 1:11 states: "This same Jesus, who was taken up from you into heaven, will so come in like manner as you saw Him go into heaven."

All of these are God's promises to you, and you can count on them. You are now a child of God, and nothing in this world can separate you from the love of God and your special place in His family.

WHAT ABOUT MY TENDENCY TO DOUBT?

Doubting is a part of human nature and does nothing to change the facts we have just outlined. You will have doubts, and your beliefs will be challenged. The real issue, then, is how you handle the doubt.

Some doubts arise to strengthen your faith or produce a deeper spiritual walk. When you have doubts, take them to God in prayer. Jesus is truth, and He is bigger than all your questions and fears. He wants to help you through those times of difficulty.

> *You will have doubts, and your beliefs will be challenged. The real issue, then, is how you handle the doubt.*

In Mark 9:14-25, we encounter the story of a dad who was emotionally distraught by the turmoil in the life of his son. He had approached the disciples and asked them to heal his son. Then he said to Jesus, "But if You can do anything, have compassion on us and help us" (v. 22).

Christ looked directly into the father's face and said, "If you can believe, all thing are possible to him who believes." The father responded by saying, "Lord, I believe; help my unbelief!" Jesus healed his son. The father was honest enough to admit his doubts and was humble enough to admit the futility of those doubts. Christ is trustworthy; the evidence of His life, teachings, miracles, character, and His death and resurrection clearly point to this. He desires a close relationship with us. Go to Him; let nothing stand in your way.

ARE ALL MY PROBLEMS OVER NOW?

Now that you have submitted yourself to Christ, you will discover that life won't necessarily be easy. The apostle Paul states that you will be "against principalities, against powers, against the rulers of the darkness of this age" (Eph. 6:12). You will be pressured daily to conform to the expectations of the world and to give in to the lusts of the flesh and the ploys of the devil. You will struggle with unhealthy desires for sex, possessions, popularity, position, and power. It will be difficult to live a life that honors Christ. However, you can have victory in all these areas.

Jesus Christ is your advocate, and He speaks daily on your behalf to God the Father (1 John 2:1-2). God will not let us be tempted beyond what we can bear; therefore, we do not stand alone in those moments when we must choose to follow Christ or give in to compromise. But we must want His help, submitting our minds, emotions, and wills to Him: "Resist the devil and he will flee from you" (James 4:7).

In addition to the abiding presence and the power of Christ, we can read, learn, and memorize the Bible, firmly planting His truth in our minds and hearts to recall in our moments of weakness. We also can rely on prayer, the indwelling Holy Spirit, the support of other Christians, and our faith in God to help us in time of need. "For whatever is born of God overcomes the world. And this is the victory that has overcome the world—our faith" (1 John 5:4).

You live in a fallen world plagued by sin, sickness, and death. Each of these will touch your life in some manner. Why we suffer is not always easy to discern. Romans 8:17 says that we must suffer in our walk of faith. No one wants to go under the surgeon's knife. But sometimes the only source of healing comes through surgery, pain, and rehabilitation. God can make us strong through suffering.

Adversity builds character and character gives evidence of Christ's work in our lives. James 1:2-4 says, "My brethren, count it all joy when you fall into various trials, knowing that the testing of your faith produces patience. But let patience have its perfect work, that you may be perfect and complete, lacking nothing." In addition, "tribulation produces perseverance; and perseverance, character; and character, hope. Now hope does not disappoint, because the love of God has been poured out in our hearts by the Holy Spirit, who was given to us" (Rom. 5:3-5). If you know that your trials are developing in you a deeper spiritual walk and a greater reliance on Christ, you will be able to see them as benefits.

WHO CAN I MODEL MY LIFE AFTER?

Jesus is our example. Get to know Him intimately by reading the Gospels. See how He modeled forgiveness, humility, reconciliation, peace, gentleness, kindness, justice, mercy, and love.

Others will disappoint you and let you down, but Christ will always meet your deepest need and guide you. Be encouraged that He loves you and came to give you a life that is abundant, rich, and full of meaning. But that's not all. He is coming to earth again. You can rest in that promise.

You are God's child. Welcome to the family!

■ GROWTH STRATEGIES ■

1. What do these verses tell you about the
    person and work of Christ?

    John 8:36

    Acts 1:11

    Acts 2:32

    Romans 5:19

    1 Peter 3:18

    1 John 2:1-2

    1 John 5:20

2. What can you learn about your
    relationship with God from these verses?

    John 1:12-13

John 14:9

Ephesians 1:7

Ephesians 1:13-14

3. What drew you to Christ? What propelled you to His mercy?

4. What are your two most pressing questions about your relationship with Christ?

5. How can you find the answers to those questions?

CHAPTER 3

RELEASING THE POWER OF THE HOLY SPIRIT

David R. Veerman
Executive Vice President,
The Livingstone Corporation

■ CHAPTER OBJECTIVE ■

For men to know, understand, and be able to release the power of the Holy Spirit.

Suppose you have just purchased a new home, the one you have been dreaming about for years, with modern kitchen appliances, a garage door opener, an intercom system, central air conditioning, a heated swimming pool, and other hi-tech amenities.

After moving in, however, you realize there is no power—you can't even turn on the lights. And so you sweat in the dark without the benefits of the wonderful equipment and appliances that are yours.

The next day your neighbor introduces himself. During the conversation, you learn that he is an electrician for the city power company. After he leaves you tell your wife about your nice neighbor. But you continue to live in a powerless house.

When it was almost time for Jesus to leave the earth He told the disciples not to fear, because they wouldn't be alone—the Father would send a "Counselor" or "Helper" to come and dwell in them (John 14:15-18). Later He said, "You shall receive power when the Holy Spirit has come upon you" (Acts 1:8). They would have all the power they would need to make the Christian life work. God's power would be available to them through the Holy Spirit. And the same is true for us today.

But the availability of power is not enough; we must plug into it. As with the electricity in the house, so it is with God's power. We must turn it on to experience it.

Think of the possibilities! God changes, heals, encourages, motivates, and equips. His power is infinite and unlimited.

> *But the availability of power is not enough; we must plug into it. We must turn it on to experience it.*

Certainly most Christians want God's power, but many just don't know how to turn it on. So the crucial question is, how can we release the Holy Spirit in our lives?

First, let's look at who the Holy Spirit is.

THE PERSON OF THE HOLY SPIRIT

Almighty God, the eternal Sovereign, Ruler of the universe is three Persons in one: Father, Son, and Holy Spirit. This is the profound doctrine of the Trinity. No matter how much we study or philosophize, we won't be able to comprehend it totally. Instead, we believe in the doctrine of the Trinity because it is taught in Scripture.

When Jesus was baptized by John the Baptist, the Bible says, "When He had been baptized, Jesus came up immediately from the water; and behold, the heavens were opened to Him, and He saw the Spirit of God descending like a dove and alighting upon Him. And suddenly a voice came from heaven, saying, 'This is My beloved Son, in whom I am well pleased' " (Matt. 3:16-17).

In this one passage, we find all three Persons of the Trinity in one place, at one time: the Father, who is speaking; the Holy Spirit, who descends; and the Son, who is being baptized. Similar situations and statements are repeated often throughout Scripture, including Matthew 28:19 (the "great commission"), Luke 1:35 (the angel's visit to Mary), and 2 Corinthians 13:14 (the "benediction").

> *Think of the Holy Spirit as God looking for a body.*

God is Father, Son, and Holy Spirit. Therefore, we use the word Trinity to describe the reality that God is three Persons. God is one in essence, with three personality centers.

Without getting too involved in a deep theological discussion, here is a simple way to understand the Trinity and the Holy Spirit. Think of the Holy Spirit as God looking for a body. Let me explain.

God the Father doesn't have a body and doesn't need one. He sustains the universe and has revealed Himself to us through the Son.

God the Son, Jesus, needed a body and has one. He needed a body to accomplish the incarnation, to be tempted just as we are and yet not sin, to suffer, to die on the cross, and to be resurrected. But because Jesus limited Himself to that body, He also limited Himself to space and time. But through the Holy Spirit, He can be everywhere, at all times. God the Son is present with us through the Holy Spirit.

> *God the Holy Spirit needs bodies. His purpose is to live inside all those who belong to God, making them Christ's body on earth.*

Stop for a moment and imagine that you had Jesus with you in the flesh. Wouldn't that be great! You could ask Him questions and introduce Him to your friends—certainly your life would change. But soon people in Connecticut would want Jesus to spend time with them . . . or people in California . . . or China. Jesus' presence would be limited by His physical body. But through the Holy Spirit, He can be (and is) with all believers, everywhere. That's why Christians are called "the body of Christ."

When you made a personal commitment to Christ as your Savior, a wonderful, life-transforming event took place. Because of what Christ did, you were declared "not guilty." You were justified; you were born into God's family;

and God Himself took up residence in your mind and heart. Right now, the Holy Spirit lives inside you.

Just like the Father and the Son, the Holy Spirit is a Person, not an "it" or an impersonal force. This means He has personality. According to the Bible, the Holy Spirit has these personal characteristics and more: He can be obeyed (Acts 10:19-21); He can be lied to (Acts 5:3); He can be resisted (Acts 7:51); He can be grieved (Eph. 4:30); He can be reverenced (Ps. 51:11); He can be blasphemed (Matt. 12:31-32); He can be outraged (Heb. 10:29).

The Holy Spirit is a Person, and this implies the possibility of personal relationship.

THE PRESENCE OF THE HOLY SPIRIT

The Bible also tells us about what the Holy Spirit does.

He Teaches

Before His crucifixion, Jesus told the disciples that the Holy Spirit would teach them and guide them into all truth (John 16:12-13). As we read the Bible, God's Word, the Holy Spirit helps us understand who Christ is, what will eventually happen to the world, and how we should live. He teaches us.

He Convicts

Any person who has felt the tug in his heart toward Christ has experienced this work of the Holy Spirit. Jesus said that the Holy Spirit would convict and convince people of sin (John

16:8). The Holy Spirit sensitizes our con-
sciences and moves us toward God.

He Guides

There is no reason for a believer in Christ to
walk around in the dark. The Holy Spirit is
there to help him understand what God wants
for his life. Romans 8:14 says, "For as many as
are led by the Spirit of God." He will give direction to those who are committed to know God's
Word, are willing to obey God, and are in fellowship with God's people.

He Helps

The Holy Spirit gives us the desire, strength,
and power to be and do what God wants (Phil.
2:12-13). He helps us love (Gal. 5:22); He helps
us know what is right (1 John 2:27); He helps
us tell others about Christ (Mark 13:11; Acts
1:8a); He even helps us pray (Rom. 8:26).

He Prepares

God, the Holy Spirit, gives us everything we
need in this world to live for Him. The "fruits
of the Spirit . . . love, joy, peace, longsuffering,
kindness, goodness, faithfulness, gentleness,
self-control" (Gal. 5:22-23). And He gives us
"spiritual gifts" for ministering to others and
for building up the rest of the body of Christ
(Rom. 12; 1 Cor. 12; Eph. 4; 1 Peter 4:10-11).

He Restrains

The only thing that keeps the world from completely unraveling is the Holy Spirit. If He
were not restraining evil today, the Holocaust

would look like a Sunday school picnic. The Holy Spirit holds back evil through direct intervention and through the lives of believers. One day, when this influence is removed, "the man of rebellion," "the son of hell" (also called the Antichrist) will rise to power (2 Thess. 2:1-12).

The Holy Spirit is working in the world and in our lives.

THE POWER OF THE HOLY SPIRIT

Now that you know a bit more about the Holy Spirit and His work, let's get back to the subject of power. You may be thinking, "It's great to know that the Holy Spirit helps people love and gives people patience. But right now, I don't feel very loving or patient. How can I experience that kind of power in my life? I want to change!"

That's a good question, and I have a simple, but profound, answer. It can be summed up with one word: commitment. Commitment means entrusting ourselves to His power, transferring control to Him, placing ourselves at His disposal, giving Him custody. Keep that word in mind as I explain the "power-process."

Perhaps you've heard people talk about receiving the Holy Spirit as though He could be discovered and held on to. And others talk about being "baptized" or being "filled" by the Spirit during a very intense, emotional experience.

> *Commitment means entrusting ourselves to His power, transferring control to Him, placing ourselves at His disposal, giving Him custody.*

Expressions like these and differing perspectives on how it all works can be very confusing. I've known many young people and adults who have searched long and hard for the Holy Spirit, and others who have tried their best to have the right experience only to be frustrated and discouraged. They can't seem to experience the Spirit.

I have no doubt that when people see God working in and through them they will say they have "found" or "discovered" the Holy Spirit. And certainly any spiritual experience can be very emotional. But the power-process isn't as difficult or as complicated as that; it's really quite simple. And it all begins with submission.

The Beginning

When you became a Christian, you *trusted* Christ; you *gave* yourself to Him; you *yielded* your life. The italicized words above are synonyms for commitment. The point is that salvation is by faith alone, not by anything we can do (Eph. 2:8-9). But trusting Christ was just the beginning. The Bible talks about being "born again" (John 3:3), and that's what happened when you made your commitment to Christ. You were born spiritually—born again into God's family. Being born is great, but it can't stop there. Any healthy newborn grows, develops, and matures.

The Process

Now you must grow, and your growth as a Christian also involves yielding. This is day-by-day and moment-by-moment commitment to God . When you accepted Christ, you gave Him "all you knew of yourself." (Jim Smith talks about this extensively in Chapter 1.) You gave Him your whole life at that time. Although it was 100 percent, you couldn't give God any more than you knew. But you are constantly growing and changing as a person. Your life today is not the same as it was when you first trusted Christ. Through reading the Bible, prayer, personal experiences, relationships, insight, and especially the Holy Spirit's work, you have learned much more about yourself. And the new you must also be given to Christ.

Colossians 2:6 says: "As you therefore have received Christ Jesus the Lord, so walk in Him." This means continually submitting areas of your life to Christ's control.

The Control

When you yield to Christ, He takes control. You've grown, and so has your faith. The point here is that Christ will not force Himself on you; He allows you to choose. But He will take over those areas that you give to Him (Rom. 6:16).

The Power

As Christ controls, the Holy Spirit's power is released in your life. This is a natural process. Remember, the Holy Spirit already lives inside you; He came in when you gave your life to Christ. Now His power is released as you continue to submit areas of your life to Christ's control (Rom. 8:12-14).

The By-Products

As the Holy Spirit's power is released in your life, wonderful by-products are produced. These include power to acknowledge Christ as Lord (1 Cor. 12:3), power to tell others about Christ (Acts 1:8), improved character (Gal. 5:22-23), a sense of knowing you are loved (Rom. 5:5), guidance (John 14:26; 16:13), sensitivity to sin (John 16:8; Eph. 4:30), and many other benefits.

In other words, through the Holy Spirit, God changes you from the inside out, making you more and more like Christ (Rom. 8:29).

The Result

It is important to remember that this is a continuing process. You are not filled with the Holy Spirit and then never again experience sin or struggle. The Holy Spirit will produce His by-products in your life, but you must continually yield to Christ and keep the process going.

Consider, for example, the by-product "sensitivity to sin." Let's say I was reading my Bible and I felt very convicted about something I had done earlier in the day (the Holy Spirit would be working in me, making me sensitive to that area in my life). In essence, I would be learning something new about myself. Right then I should talk to God and yield that area to Him, asking for forgiveness and direction. Then Christ would control that area, and the Holy Spirit would empower me in that area, and the growth process would continue.

If, however, you choose to stop yielding or to ignore the Holy Spirit's prodding, you will experience guilt, lack of power, and the loss of the other by-products. In effect, the power-process will be short-circuited.

The Point

This is a natural process. The Holy Spirit works in you, and His power changes you as you continue to submit to Christ. You can't ever work hard enough to receive His power— it doesn't come by works. You can't ever work up enough emotion or devotion to receive His power—it doesn't come by feelings. You can't get the Holy Spirit by trying to find Him or grab hold of Him.

I once heard some young people singing, "I want more of Jesus, more and more and more. I want more of Jesus than I ever had before." Although their motives were right, I believe they had it turned around. Instead of wanting more of Jesus or the Spirit, we should be giving Him more and more of us. Then He will give us all we need of Him.

The Holy Spirit is looking for a body. His power and all His by-products are yours as you

commit yourself to Him. Why live in the dark?
Turn on His power!

■ GROWTH STRATEGIES ■

1. What do these passages teach about the
    Holy Spirit?

    John 14:15-18

    John 16:8-11

    John 16:12-13

    Acts 1:8

    Romans 8:26

    1 Corinthians 12:4-11

    Galatians 5:22-23

2. How has God changed you since you
    became a Christian?

3. Through Bible study, church, relationships, and personal experiences, what has God been teaching you about yourself? In other words, what new information have you learned about yourself lately?

4. What area do you find difficult to submit to Christ's control?

5. What hinders you from committing this area to Christ?

6. What can you do to release the Holy Spirit's power in that area of your life (pray, obey, ask for help)?

7. List your available spiritual resources (family, clergy, books, seminars, videos, church programs).

CHAPTER 4

THE BIBLE: TRUSTWORTHINESS AND IMPORTANCE

Dr. R.C. Sproul
Theologian, speaker, and author

■ CHAPTER OBJECTIVE ■

To relate the importance of the Bible and Bible study and to encourage men to take seriously the Word of God revealed in Scripture.

First, let's look at some reasons people give for not studying the Bible. These "reasons" often contain myths that are passed off as truths through constant repetition. The myth I hear most often is this:

MYTH #1:   *Only highly skilled theologians with technical training can deal with the Scriptures.*

This myth has been repeated many times by sincere people. They say, "I know I can't study the Bible, because every time I try to read it, I can't understand it." When they express this myth, they do it with astonishing ease. The myth is so familiar that they do not expect it to be challenged. Yet the fact is that as mature adults, living in the United States of America, having a high school education or better, we can understand the basic message of the Bible. If we can read the newspaper, we can read the Bible. In fact, I would venture to guess that more difficult words and concepts are expressed on the front page of a newspaper than on most pages of the Bible.

A kernel of truth behind this myth may involve the particular Bible a person has tried to read. The aged family Bible with four hundred-year-old English is written in a different language than you speak. Make sure you have an up-to-date Bible to study.

MYTH #2: *The Bible is boring.*

When we press people for an explanation of what they mean when they express the first myth, usually they respond by saying, "Well, I guess I can understand a lot of it, but frankly the book bores me to death." Passing by for a moment the miracle that the speaker is still living, we note that the problem is no longer that the Bible is difficult, but that it is dull.

When people imply that the Bible is dull, I wonder why. Biblical characters are full of life. There is a unique quality of passion about them. Their lives reveal drama, pathos, lust, crime, devotion and every conceivable aspect of human existence. There is rebuke, remorse, contrition, consolation, practical wisdom, philosophical reflection and, most of all, truth. Perhaps the dullness of some experience is due to the arrogant assumption that what is ancient cannot possibly be interesting or relevant. The question might be asked, "How does the life of Abraham—lived so long ago and far away—relate to us?" The answer is, by remembering that the characters of biblical history are real. Though their life settings are different from ours, their struggles and concerns are very much like ours.

The myths actually uncover two dangerous tendencies in us. We desire our spiritual food, like most of our nourishment, fast and spoon-fed. We neglect the truth that satisfaction is directly related to willing effort. There are probably several enjoyable activities in your life right now that became so because you invested time and effort to master them. Doesn't God's Word deserve at least that much attention?

THE CLARITY OF SCRIPTURE

In the sixteenth century, the Reformers declared their total confidence in what they called the "perspicuity" of Scripture. What they meant by that technical term was the clarity of Scripture. They maintained that the Bible is basically clear and lucid. Its message is simple enough for any literate person to understand. This is not to say that all parts of the Bible are equally clear or that there are no difficult passages to be found in it. Laymen unskilled in the more technical aspects of Bible study may have difficulty with sections of Scripture, but the message of salvation is apparent throughout. Luther, for example, was convinced that what was obscure in one part of Scripture would be understood in some other part of Scripture.

If you have clung to the myths of dullness or difficulty, perhaps it's because you have attributed to the whole of Scripture what you have found in some of its parts. Maybe some passages have been peculiarly difficult. Other passages have left you bewildered and baffled. Perhaps those should be left for later, or for scholars to unravel. If you find certain portions of the Bible beyond you, need you insist that the whole of Scripture is boring and dull? Most sports are played and enjoyed long before all their complexities or rules are fully understood.

THE BIBLICAL BASIS FOR BIBLE STUDY

The Bible itself is straightforward in declaring the importance of our study of its words. Let us examine two passages, one from each Testament, in order to catch a glimpse of these mandates.

In Deuteronomy 6 we find an Old Testament passage that was familiar to every Jew. Its words were used to call the assembly together for worship. We read: "Hear, O Israel: The Lord our God, the Lord is one! You shall love the Lord your God with all your heart, with all your soul, and with all your might" (vv. 4-5). It turns out most of us are familiar with these words. But what follows them immediately? Read on: "And these words which I command you today shall be in your heart. You shall teach them diligently to your children, and shall talk of them when you sit in your house, when you walk by the way, when you lie down, and when you rise up. You shall bind them as a sign on your hand, and they shall be as front-lets between your eyes. You shall write them on the doorposts of your house and on your gates" (vv. 6-9).

God's sovereign command is that His Word be taught so diligently that it penetrates the heart. The content of that Word is not to be mentioned casually and infrequently. Repeated discussion is the order of the day, every

day. The call to bind on the hand, the fore-
head, the doorpost, and the gate makes it clear
that God is insisting that His Word be studied
by whatever method it takes. The expressions
may be unfamiliar, but they make sense if we
say that God wants the Bible "close at hand,
on our minds, and posted on our walls."

> *God's sovereign command is that His
> Word be taught so diligently that
> it penetrates the heart.*

Turning to the New Testament, we read Paul's
admonition to Timothy: "But you must continue in the things which you have learned
and been assured of, knowing from whom you
have learned them, and that from childhood
you have known the Holy Scriptures, which
are able to make you wise for salvation
through faith which is in Christ Jesus. All
Scripture is given by inspiration of God, and is
profitable for doctrine, for reproof, for correction, for instruction in righteousness; that the
man of God may be complete, thoroughly
equipped for every good work" (2 Tim. 3:14-17).

This exhortation is so basic to our understanding of the importance of Bible study that each
phrase warrants careful scrutiny.

". . . continue in the things which you have
learned . . ." (v. 14). Our study of Scripture
must be a consistent matter. There is no room
for the proverbial "once over lightly" approach.
A persistent decision to grow in learning is a
key part of the right attitude for Bible study.

". . . the Holy Scriptures, which are able to make you wise for salvation . . ." (v. 15). When the Bible speaks of "wisdom," it refers to the practical matter of learning how to live a life that is pleasing to God. Wisdom in the highest sense, then, is being wise with respect to salvation ". . . through faith which is in Christ Jesus" (v. 15). Paul is saying that through the Scriptures we can acquire that kind of wisdom that concerns our ultimate fulfillment and destiny as human beings.

"All Scripture is given by inspiration of God . . ." (v. 16). Volumes of theological literature have focused on this passage. The crucial word in the passage is the Greek term theopneust, which is often translated "inspired by God." This literally means "God-breathed," which refers not so much to God's breathing something "in" as to His breathing something "out." Rather than the term "inspiration," it might be better to render the Greek by the English "expiration." In that case we would see the significance of the passage not so much in providing us with a theory of inspiration—a theory of how God transmitted His Word through human authors—but rather a statement of the origin or source of Scripture. What Paul is saying to Timothy is that the Bible comes from God. He is its ultimate author. It is His word, carrying with it the weight of all that He is. Thus, the injunction to remember ". . . from whom you have learned them [these things]" (v. 14).

"All Scripture . . . is profitable for doctrine [teaching] . . ." (v. 16). Paul now mentions some preeminent ways in which the Bible profits us. The first and foremost profit is that the Bible is our teacher. We may pick up the Bible and be "inspired" and moved to tears or feel other poignant emotions. But our greatest profit is in being instructed. The instruction is not about everything, but about the most important things; the things of God. This instruction is called "profitable" because God Himself places an extremely high value on it. The instruction is assigned worth and significance.

"All Scripture is . . . profitable . . . for reproof, correction, and instruction in righteousness" (v. 16). In these words Paul articulates the practical value of Bible study. As fallen creatures we sin, we err, and we are inherently out of shape with respect to righteousness. When we sin, we need to be "reproved." When we err, we need to be "corrected." When we are out of shape, we need to go into "training." The Scriptures function as our chief reprover, our chief corrector, and our chief trainer. There is no shortage of books written to teach excellence in almost every area of life. They all claim to be profitable for training readers in particular skills. But where are the books that will train us in righteousness? All those other books cannot answer the question, "For what profit is it to a man if he gains the whole world, and loses his own soul?" (Matt. 16:26).

". . . That the man of God may be complete, thoroughly equipped for every good work" (v. 17). The Christian who is not diligently involved in a serious study of Scripture is simply incomplete as a disciple of Christ. To be a "complete" Christian and adequate in the things of God, one must do more than attend "sharing sessions" and "bless me parties." We cannot learn competency by osmosis. The biblically illiterate Christian is not only inadequate but ill-equipped. In fact, he is inadequate because he is ill-equipped. Lee Trevino may be able to put on incredible exhibitions of his prodigious skill by hitting golf balls with a taped-up Dr. Pepper bottle. But he doesn't use a Dr. Pepper bottle off the tee in the U.S. Open.

THE BIBLE AS REVELATION

The Bible also deserves our study because it provides information that is not available anywhere else. Our universities provide us with a wealth of knowledge acquired by human investigation of the natural world. We learn by observation, analysis, and abstract speculation. These are, however, all limited efforts. Only God can provide us with an eternal perspective and speak to us with absolute and final authority. If He did not wish to reveal Himself to us, we would know nothing about Him. But He did wish to reveal Himself to us—partly though His creation, personally through His Son, Jesus, and also through His written Word.

The Scriptures do, of course, talk of matters that can be learned by other means. We are not utterly dependent on the New Testament to learn who Caesar Augustus was or how far it is from Jerusalem to Bethany. But the world's best geographer cannot show us the way to God, and the world's best psychiatrist cannot give us a final answer to the problem of guilt. There are matters contained in the Bible that unveil for us that which is not exposed to the natural course of human investigation.

> *Only God can provide us with an eternal perspective and speak to us with absolute and final authority.*

When we speak about the concept of revelation we are talking about the basic principle of self-disclosure. The Scriptures come to us as divine self-disclosure. Here the mind of God is shown clearly on many matters. With a knowledge of Scripture we do not have to rely on second-hand information or bare speculation to learn who God is and what He values. In the Bible He reveals Himself.

THEORY AND PRACTICE

There are those who despise any quest for theoretical knowledge of God, insisting instead on being "practical." In fact, the spirit of America has been defined as the spirit of pragmatism. Pragmatism may be defined simply as the approach to reality that sees truth as "that which works." The pragmatist is concerned about results, and the results determine the truth. The problem with this kind of thinking, if left uninformed by the eternal perspective, is that the results tend to be judged solely in terms of short-term goals.

The person who concerns himself only with short-term goals may have big trouble when it comes to the very long run of eternity. Practicality is always based on some underlying theory, even if it is unconscious. The person who despises theory but still calls himself practical is not wise. We do what we do because we have a theory about the value of doing it. Nothing betrays our deepest theories more eloquently than our actions. We may never think seriously about our theories or subject them to rigorous critical analysis, but we all have them. The person who wants practicality without theory will usually wind up with bad theories that will in turn lead to bad practices.

> *Nothing could be more practical than God's Word because its theories are established from the eternal perspective.*

Because the theories found in Scripture proceed from God, the Bible is eminently practical. Nothing could be more practical than God's Word because its theories are established from the eternal perspective. The fatal weakness of pragmatism is overcome by revelation. God gives us in the Bible what we could never find out on our own.

THE BIBLE AND YOUR MIND

The Bible is addressed primarily, though not exclusively, to our understanding. That means the mind. This is difficult to communicate to modern Christians who are living in what may be the most anti-intellectual period of Western civilization. Notice, I did not say anti-academic or anti-technological or anti-scholarly. I said anti-intellectual. There is a strong current of mistrust toward the function of the mind in the Christian life.

Christianity is supremely intellectual though not intellectualistic. That is, Scripture is addressed to the intellect without at the same time embracing a spirit of intellectualism. The mind is respected and used, but not revered. The Christian life is not to be a life of bare conjecture or cold rationalism; it is to be a life of vibrant passion. Strong feelings of joy, love, and exaltation are called for again and again. But those passionate feelings are a response to what we understand with our minds to be true. When we read in Scripture, "But be of good cheer, I have overcome the world" (John 16:33). "ho-hum" is not an appropriate response. We can be of good cheer because we understand that Christ has indeed overcome the world. That thrills our souls and sets our feet to dancing. What is more precious than to experience the sweetness of the presence of Christ or the nearness of the Holy Spirit?

> *We must do what God says, like it or not.*
> *That is what Christianity is all about.*

God forbid that we should lose our passion or go through the Christian pilgrimage without any experience of Christ. But what happens when there is a conflict between what God says and what I feel? We must do what God says, like it or not. That is what Christianity is all about.

Reflect for a moment. What happens in your life when you act according to what you feel like doing rather than what you know and understand God says you should do? Here we encounter the ruthless reality of the difference between happiness and pleasure. How easy it is to confuse the two! The pursuit of happiness is regarded as our inalienable right. But happiness and pleasure are not the same thing. Both of them feel good, but only one endures. Sins may bring pleasure, but never happiness. If sin were not so pleasurable, it would hardly represent a temptation. Yet, while sin often "feels good," it does not produce happiness. If we do not know the difference, or worse yet, do not care about the difference, we are in big trouble.

It is precisely at the point of discerning the difference between pleasure and happiness that knowledge of Scripture is so vital. There is a remarkable relationship between God's will and human happiness. The fundamental deception of Satan is the lie that obedience can never bring happiness. From the primordial temptation of Adam and Eve to last night's satanic seduction, the lie has been the same: "If you do what God says, you will not be happy. If you do what I say, you will be 'liberated' and know happiness."

If there is a secret, a carefully guarded secret, to human happiness, it is the one expressed in a seventeenth-century catechism that says, "Man's chief end is to glorify God and to enjoy Him forever." The secret to happiness is found in obedience to God. How can we be happy if we are not obedient? How can we be obedient if we do not know what it is we are to obey? Thus, the top and the tail of it is that happiness cannot be fully discovered as long as we remain ignorant of God's Word.

To be sure, knowledge of God's Word does not guarantee that we will do what it says, but at least we will know what we are supposed to be doing in our quest for human fulfillment.

> *The issue of faith is not so much whether we believe in God, but whether we believe the God we believe in.*

A MATTER OF DUTY

Why should we study the Bible? We have mentioned briefly the practical value, the ethical importance, and the way of happiness. We have looked at some of the myths that are given to explain, or excuse, why people do not study the Bible. We have examined something of the spirit of pragmatism and the anti-intellectual climate of our day. There are many facets to the question and countless reasons we ought to study the Bible.

I could plead with you to study the Bible for personal edification. I could try the art of persuasion to stimulate your quest for happiness. I could say that the study of the Bible would probably be the most fulfilling and rewarding educational experience of your life. I could cite numerous reasons you would benefit from a serious study of Scripture. But ultimately the main reason we should study the Bible is because it is our duty.

Even if the Bible were the most boring book in the world, dull, uninteresting, and seemingly irrelevant, it would still be our duty to study it. If its literary style were awkward and confusing, the duty would remain. We live as human beings under an obligation by divine mandate to study diligently God's Word. He is our Sovereign, it is His Word, and He commands that we study it. A duty is not an option.

Taken from *Knowing Scripture* by R.C. Sproul. Copyright 1977 by InterVarsity Christian Fellowship of the USA. Used by permission of InterVarsity Press, P.O. Box 1400, Downers Grove, IL 60515.

■ GROWTH STRATEGIES ■

1. What do these passages teach about the
    importance of the Bible?

    Deuteronomy 6:4-9

    1 Corinthians 2:12-13

    Philippians 1:9-11

    2 Timothy 3:14-17

    2 Peter 1:20-21

2. What convinces you that the Bible is the
    Word of God?

3.   Why is it important to study God's Word?

4.   What is the main reason you use for putting off studying the Bible?

5.   What steps can you take to understand the Bible more clearly?

6.   What practical steps could you take to improve your Bible study?

THE TOOL LIST: BIBLE STUDY BASICS

Invest a lunch hour in your spiritual education. Near your work place there should be a Christian bookstore. Visit, ask questions, and examine the following essential tools for Bible study.

Bible—Before you look at Bibles, find out from three or four Christians whom you admire which Bible translation they find most useful. Ask your pastor too. It's also a great way to break the ice at the next Gathering of Men breakfast—tell those at your table you're looking for a Bible and would be interested in their recommendations.

When you get to the store, you will probably be astounded by the variety and price range. Ask to see the ones on your list. Open each one to the same place and read the same verses to determine which version is the most natural for you.

Once you have chosen a Bible version, you will have to decide on binding, type, and included helps. Don't buy a study Bible unless the extras really help you. Don't just take the salesperson's word for it. Look at the "helps"—charts, indexes, maps, notes. Do they help you?

Dictionary—There are several good Bible dictionaries that will give you an overview of subjects you will run across in your study. Look up several names or terms (salvation, church, sacrifice, Jonah) to decide whether it would be helpful to you.

> *Concordance*—These books, now available on computer, list a word and every occurrence of it in the Bible. They are helpful in tracking down different uses of a word, or different places where the same subject is discussed. Be sure to get one based on the particular version of the Bible you are buying.

BIBLE STUDY: GETTING STARTED

There are many books that can help you with Bible study. Your pastor or a friend from The Gathering of Men may be able to recommend a good one. In the meantime, these ideas should get you started.

When you were in school, you probably discovered a method of study that worked for you. Keep that in mind as you approach the Bible. The way you managed to study and understand Geometry and Biology will help you study your Bible.

Since Christianity is all about Christ, you should start with one of His biographies—the four Gospels (Matthew, Mark, Luke or John). Eventually you will want to be familiar with all four, but here is a way to choose which one to start with:

If you like action, start with Mark. If you like history, start with Luke. If you like words, start with John. If you like culture, start with Matthew.

Read at a speed that allows you to understand. Don't skip over questions your mind brings up.

Some beginners take the fishing approach—read 'till you get a bite. A bite is a challenge to your life, a new idea, a command you need to obey, or a passage that makes you think.

Others take a more systematic approach. They read a paragraph or a chapter at a time and ask themselves some standard clarifying questions. Here are two ways to analyze what you are reading. They can be remembered easily by their first letters.

S.T.E.P.S.: *after you read a passage,*

*S*top long enough to see what it says.

*T*hink long enough to discover what it means.

*E*valuate to ask what God wants you to do.

*P*lan a personal response to what you learn.

*S*tart the action you decide to take.

or

A.B.C.: *after each passage, take time for,*

*A*nalysis—try to say it in your own words.

*B*est verse—find one key idea to remember.

*C*hallenge—decide what the passage requires of you.

There are many other methods you will discover along the way. The important thing is to get started!

Remember, you are seeking to learn, to grow in knowledge. But you are not just filling up. The truth has to flow through you. No real learning is taking place until you apply it.

CHAPTER 5

PRAYER

Dr. Leighton Ford
Leighton Ford Ministries

■ CHAPTER OBJECTIVE ■

*To help you learn to "practice the presence of
Christ" in your own life, through prayer.*

Samuel Johnson, the great English writer, was
once asked what was the best argument for
prayer. "Sir," he replied, "there is no argument
for prayer." Johnson didn't mean that prayer is
useless, but that it is so much a part of our nature that we can't help but pray.

About three hundred years ago there lived in
Paris a wonderful Christian named Brother
Lawrence. He was a cook in the Carmelite
Monastery. Brother Lawrence used to talk
about "practicing the presence of Christ." He
would say, "God is here, close beside me; and
He is everywhere, so that I can never again be
out of His holy presence." To Brother Lawrence, his kitchen was as holy as a church. To
many others, his kitchen became a place where
they could meet God.

Both of the statements you just read describe
prayer, but they are actually far apart. Johnson described the human starting point: everybody "prays"—sometimes! We don't have to be
convinced to do this kind of praying. Instead

we get cornered into it by life's difficulties. But if this is the extent of our communication with God, He gradually becomes to us a god of crises, instead of the Lord of life. God gets filed between "F" for furnace repair and "I" for Insurance—people we only talk to when we need them. There is tremendous growth in the Christian life between Johnson's starting point and Brother Lawrence's description of prayer as a constant awareness of and communication with God. Most of us spend too much time practicing prayer as an occasional necessity and too little time experiencing the presence of Christ.

A DAILY QUIET TIME

One of the great secrets for growing up in Christ is to remember that whether we're riding a bus or working in the office or washing dishes at home or playing a game of golf, Jesus Christ is there. He said, "I am with you always, even to the end of the age" (Matt: 28:20). So, if Christ promised to be "with us" always, how can we be with Him?

> *One of the great secrets for growing up in Christ is to remember that whether we're riding a bus or working in the office or washing dishes at home or playing a game of golf, Jesus Christ is there.*

To help you learn to "practice the presence of Christ" in your own life, I'd like to suggest that the most valuable habit you can develop is to set aside a "quiet time" every day to be with

God. Even though it's true that Christ is with you at all times and in all places, still I have found, and I believe that all growing Christians have, that we need to set aside a special time with Him to help us be more conscious of Him the rest of the time.

Let me share my own experience. I first opened my heart to the Lord Jesus Christ when I was a small boy. But I didn't really grow in my Christian life until my mid-teens. At a summer youth conference, I heard a minister tell about his "morning watch." To be frank, I didn't feel like watching much of anything in the morning! But I was fascinated as he told how, being a nervous person, he didn't kneel down when he prayed, but walked back and forth. He prayed out loud so that his thoughts wouldn't wander. To keep his prayers fresh, he would read a passage of Scripture and turn it into a prayer. Somehow, as I listened to him, the truth was brought home to me that God actually wanted fellowship with me. The next morning I went out into the woods with my Bible and for the first time consciously sought to have fellowship with God.

I find that when I meet with God in this quiet time, it brings me strength, peace, and a sense of direction, purpose, and dedication for the day. Because of its effect in my own life, I encourage you to develop a habit of quiet time with God.

I would suggest that right now you plan when and how you're going to have this time with the Lord. If at all possible, find a room where you can be alone. (If necessary, buy an alarm clock and get up a bit earlier in the morning!) Some people prefer to have their quiet time before breakfast. I find that my mind is clearer if I've had breakfast first. (But I must confess that after breakfast there is a real temptation to get into business, correspondence, and reading of the newspaper, and to let the quiet time be crowded out!)

Set a reasonable length of time, but not too long at first. One mistake I made was to have an hour-long quiet time the first two mornings, only to find that it was too long, and I let it drop altogether. In fact, you might begin with just ten minutes a day.

You could use those ten minutes in the following way:

Take one minute to remind yourself that you're going into the presence of God Himself. You wouldn't rush breathlessly into an audience with a head of state. We ought to prepare our hearts and minds to realize what a great and wonderful privilege it is to be with God.

Use the next five minutes to read a passage of Scripture. Before you read the Scripture, use this prayer from the Psalms: "Open my eyes to see wondrous things from Your law" (Ps. 119:18). Read carefully and thoughtfully through the passage for the day. My wife and I often read together from a little selection of Scripture readings called Daily Light, which you can find in most Christian bookstores. And we have read through The Living Bible together.

> *Take one minute to remind yourself that you're going into the presence of God Himself.*

Spend the remainder of your time in prayer. Ask the Lord to help you apply the truths you've found in your Scripture reading. Plan your day with Him, and ask Him to guide you.

Ten minutes spent this way every day will not only make a difference in your life, it will convince you that ten minutes is not enough time to spend with God. Remember: the objective is to "practice the presence of Christ."

QUIET TIME PRAYER

Like any encounter with a loved one, you can see that a quiet time should include two interwoven strands: receiving and responding. We receive from God by allowing Him to speak to us through His Word, the Bible. (Elsewhere in this book, you will read about the overall importance of the Bible as God's Word, but here I am suggesting that during quiet time you use the Bible to listen more than study.) We respond to God through prayer. Prayer happens naturally when we really listen to God. Here's what Jesus said about prayer.

Jesus tells us in the Sermon on the Mount, "Ask, and it will be given to you; seek, and you will find; knock, and it will be opened to you" (Matt: 7-7). It sounds as if prayer equals asking. But prayer is more than that; it is a matter of our very being.

The devotional writer, Oswald Chambers, said, "Prayer is not getting things from God . . . prayer is getting into perfect communion with God; I tell Him what I know He knows in order that I may get to know it as He does." And again Chambers writes, "Prayer is not only asking, it is an attitude of heart that produces an atmosphere in which asking is perfectly natural."

Look carefully again at Jesus' words: "Ask, and it will be given to you; seek, and you will find; knock, and it will be opened to you. For everyone who asks receives, he who seeks finds, and to him who knocks it will be opened. Or what man is there among you, who if his son asks for bread, will give him a stone? Or if he asks for a fish, will he give him a serpent? If you then, being evil, know how to give good gifts to your children, how much more will your Father who is in heaven give good things to those who ask Him!" (vv. 7-11).

What does Jesus teach us here about prayer?

Prayer is recognizing that I have a need: "Ask . . ." It is recognizing that I have needs for bread, clothing, and shelter and for His Holy Spirit. As a human being I am not self-sufficient; I am incomplete and insufficient. So I must ask.

Prayer is recognizing that what I receive are gifts. "Ask, and it will be given . . ." The things I ask for are not rights or rewards. They are gifts to be sought, not earned.

Prayer reflects a persistent spirit. Jesus' words can be translated, "Keep on asking, keep on seeking, keep on knocking." Prayer is a desire that grows in strength. Thus, the ascending scale: asking, seeking, knocking. Notice how this moves from the easiest to the hardest. I may ask you for something that is right next to you. I may go seeking for something that is in another room. But I may have to go some distance and knock on the door of another house for something that is not at hand. So prayer is active, not passive!

> **Prayer is a habit of the heart.**

Prayer is a habit of the heart. "Everyone who asks" could be translated "every asker receives." Prayer is what I am, not just what I do. True prayer becomes part of our very character. Remember what Chambers said: Prayer is "an attitude of the heart that produces an atmosphere in which asking is perfectly natural."

Prayer is supernaturally natural. "What man is there among you who, if his son asks for bread, will give him a stone?" As children we know how to ask. As parents we know how to give. So prayer takes a natural instinct and gives it a supra-natural orientation. "How much more will your Father who is in heaven . . . ?"

Calvin Thielman, a Presbyterian pastor, has been a friend of mine for many years. Some years ago he was in the hospital with a serious kidney problem. I went to pray with him. He held my hand and said, "Leighton, it bothers me that I hurt so much that I can't even pray. I can just tell God that I hurt and say, 'God, help me.'"

I asked him, "Calvin, if your little son, Sam, was sick and all he could say was 'Daddy, I hurt,' would he need to say anything else?"

So, prayer is also a relationship. "How much more will your Father . . . give?" Prayer is the speaking part of our relationship with our Father. It leads to greater intimacy with Him. If I don't talk to my wife and my children, we won't have much of a relationship. We can often be near each other without talking, but when we do talk, our words reflect our total relationship. The same is true of our relationship with God.

Learning to talk to God is like learning to talk when we are babies. If parents anticipate a baby's every need, handing him things before he asks, the baby will never learn to talk. If they wait until the young child begins to say his words, however garbled, the child learns to express himself. Later, parents and child can talk back and forth on a more grown-up level.

Asking is an important part of learning to converse so that a relationship can grow. We never get to the place where we don't need to ask. But we ought to grow to the place where we do more than ask.

Prayer is a strong trust in the wisdom, goodness, and power of our Father. He knows what we need before we ask Him (Matt. 6:8). He knows how to give good gifts to those who ask Him (Matt. 7:11). God's wisdom knows what is best for us, His goodness wills what is best, and His power provides what is best.

Thus, prayer is an honor to my Father, not a presumption or an inconvenience. As author Tim Stafford puts it, "We do not pray to tell God what He does not know, nor to remind Him of things He has forgotten. When we pray, we stand by God and look with Him toward these people and problems . . . we express our faith in Him . . . none of this is news to our Heavenly Father. We speak to Him as we speak to our most intimate friends."

THE RESULTS OF PRAYER

Based on Jesus' words about prayer, what attitudes toward life does prayer nurture? Some would criticize prayer as something that encourages people to be gullible, naive, neurotic, and passive. There have been thousands of others, however, who have found in these words of Jesus the very keys to "practicing the presence of Christ."

Which result seems more likely from what we've learned about prayer? Are the attitudes that prayer nurtures healthy or unhealthy? Consider the following attitudes.

If prayer is recognizing that I have needs, then prayer brings an attitude of humility rather than pride.

If the things I receive are gifts, then prayer expresses a grateful heart.

If prayer reflects a persistent spirit, then it creates an attitude of enterprise and responsibility rather than fatalism or a need to control everything.

If prayer is supra-natural, allowing us to see our day-by-day relationships from a godly perspective, then prayer allows us to be open to the eternal as well as the temporal.

If prayer is the speaking part of our relationship with God, it ought to cultivate open communication with others and make us people who share our needs and gifts.

If prayer creates intimacy with God, it ought to bring warmth to all of our relationships.

If prayer is trust, then it ought to root our lives in confidence rather than worry, cynicism, and doubt.

And if prayer is an attitude of honor to our Creator, our Father in heaven, then the more we pray the more we should become reverent people toward God, others, and life itself.

This is how a friend describes her growing relationship with God: "Prayer has become more and more a way of life. I pray about everything. It has become a desire and delight—not something I do out of obligation or even out of obedience." Doesn't that sound like she's learned something of what it means to practice the presence of Christ?

HOW TO PRAY

Here are some practical suggestions on how to pray effectively. I suggest to some people this simple acrostic:

A—Adoration
C—Confession
T—Thanksgiving
S—Supplication and Submission

This forms the word ACTS. Our prayers should begin with adoration of God for who He is, move on to confession of our sins, thanksgiving for God's blessings, and supplication for our needs and the needs of others, and end with submission as we commit ourselves and our day into His hands.

You may wish to visualize the Cross in your mind as you pray. That reminds us that only through Christ's death do we have the privilege of coming to God. Let the top point of the Cross remind you of adoration; the bottom point, of confession; the center, of thanksgiving; the left arm, of supplication; and the right arm, of submission.

> *God's greatest concern is not the length of our prayers, nor the correctness of our language, but the attitude of our hearts.*

Don't limit your prayers to a formal act once a day. Get in the habit of sending "flash" prayers to God many times each day. Pray when you wake up; pray before meals; pray as you walk or ride or wait; pray when you can't sleep. Doing your work or enjoying recreation to the glory of God can be a prayer! We can pray even without closing our eyes or kneeling. It is essential, however, that we make time each day to discipline ourselves to talk to God and listen to Him.

Most important of all, remember that prayer is conversation with God. God's greatest concern is not the length of our prayers, nor the correctness of our language, but the attitude of our hearts. As Jesus said, "God is Spirit, and those who worship Him must worship in spirit and truth" (John 4:24).

Start each day by tilting the mirror of your soul toward God, and then ask Him to reflect His reality through you to others. As your awareness of Him fills the hours of the day, you will be practicing the presence of Christ.

Portions of this chapter have been adapted from a chapter in *Letters to a New Christian* by Leighton Ford: copyright 1987 by World Wide Publications, Minneapolis, Minnesota. Used by permission.

■ GROWTH STRATEGIES ■

1. Based on the following verses, what is important to keep in mind about prayer?

    Matthew 6:6-7

    Matthew 7:7

    Matthew 7:8-11

    Mark 14:38

    Philippians 4:6

    1 Thessalonians 5:17

    James 5:13-14

    James 5:16

2. When did you last spend at least two
    minutes in prayer? What did you talk to
    God about? Why did you decide to pray?

3. How do you feel about setting aside time
    each day to pray?

4. What barriers might keep you from
    praying?

5. What is the best time for you to pray?

    _____ in the morning

    _____ commuting to and from work

    _____ in the evening

    _____ other

6. Try using the ACTS method for three
    weeks. List what you could talk to God
    about in each category.

    A

    C

    T

    S

Personal and Progressive Commitment in Your Relationship with Self

CHAPTER 6

SUCCESS

Adolph Coors IV
Investment Counselor and Speaker

■ CHAPTER OBJECTIVE ■

When you finish this chapter, I hope you will be able to incorporate God's standards of success into your world.

A successful man was asked the secret of his accomplishments. He replied, "Good judgment." Then he was asked, "Where did you learn good judgment, sir?" The man answered, "From experience." "Where did you gain your experience, sir?" He replied, "From poor judgment."

I think he had the right idea. If we are willing to learn from our mistakes, we can find success.

Let me share a true story about a man who came to grips in a rather hard fashion with the nature of true success. This was a businessman like you and me. I'll change his name to George Smith.

George Smith wanted to become the president of his company. He worked hard, and after many years he built a successful national sales organization. The day came when Mr. Smith became the president of his company. He was at the top. He was very proud, and he thought he had achieved true happiness and success. But it was short-lived.

Things began to fall apart for Mr. Smith. Business declined dramatically. First, he had to close the New York office, then the Chicago office. His newly-acquired empire began to crumble around him, and he saw himself losing everything he had given his life to. Finally, the terrible day came when he had to close his last office. Here's how George Smith tells his story.

"I locked the door of my office for the final time. Never in all my life had I felt so low as when I turned my back on my broken dreams. I walked slowly to the parking lot, got into my car, and headed for home. What was my wife going to think when I walked in the door early in the day and broke the news?

"I entered the house as I had done many times before at the end of a busy day, expecting my wife to call out, 'Honey is that you? Are you home?' On this day, however, the house was silent. I walked into the kitchen and saw a note pinned to the refrigerator: 'I've gone to the store. I'll be home late.'

"I sank into my favorite easy chair, crushed in spirit. Suddenly the kitchen door flew open—it was my little girl home from school. She put her lunch box on the kitchen table, pausing just long enough to notice me in the living room. 'You're home early; how come Daddy?'

"Well, I didn't want to hear that. I didn't want to discuss it right then, so I just said, 'Honey, Daddy is changing jobs right now. But let's not talk about it.'

"Then she jumped into my lap, hugged me tight around my neck, pressing her soft warm face against mine, and gave me the sweetest kiss, saying, 'Daddy, oh Daddy; I love you so much.'

"That did it. I began to cry. 'What's wrong Daddy? What's wrong?'

"And I said, 'Honey, nothing. Nothing at all. There's absolutely nothing wrong.'

"And you know, I really meant it. In that brief moment, I suddenly discovered, for the first time, that I had all I really wanted. In an instant, my life unfolded before my eyes. As a young fellow I wanted to be great and have success in order to be recognized. I thought that I needed this success to be important, to feel needed by my peers, to be loved and respected by my family.

"As I sat in my living room that afternoon, I knew that I actually had what was truly important. It was right there on my lap. I was loved; and in being loved, I found my sense of self-respect and my dignity."

George Smith realized that to succeed in the eyes of man but to fail in the eyes of God is the ultimate waste.

WHAT IS SUCCESS?

The American Heritage Dictionary defines success this way: 1. the achievement of something desired 2. the gaining of fame and prosperity 3. the achievement of wealth or eminence.

The world judges success from a public standpoint. A person may do work that is fulfilling, earn enough money to meet the family's needs, be respected by friends and loved by family, enjoy good health, have peace of mind, die at a ripe old age and be mourned at death, and yet be considered a total failure in the eyes of the world if he or she has not achieved great fame, fortune or power.

Consider the reverse. A person may have achieved remarkable success because of his public impact and yet be a miserable failure in his private life. Public success, as the world judges, has nothing to do with a person's emotions, intimate relationships, or character qualities.

> *Public success, as the world judges, has nothing to do with a person's emotions, intimate relationships, or character qualities.*

Dennis Rainey, founder and director of the family ministry of Campus Crusade for Christ, has said, "Today, tough questions face businessmen and leaders. Who should be our role models? We worship successful pro athletes and successful businessmen who can perform in the corporate boardrooms of America and perform on Saturday and Sunday on the gridiron and the athletic fields across this country. But you and I don't give a rip about what they are in private life. We don't care to dig any deeper than what we see on the surface."

Success and public impact are judged entirely by superiority and beauty, considering such things as popularity, fame, influence, political power, wealth, talent, and creativity. These are the marks of success in the world's eyes.

But all of us are mere mortals. All of us are fallen descendants of Adam and Eve. That makes us egocentric sinners. It means that pride motivates us to exhibit and exercise our superiority so that we may be noticed and applauded, preferably with a bigger pay check.

The apostle John writes in 1 John 2:16: "For all that is in the world—the lust of the flesh, the lust of the eyes, and the pride of life—is not of the Father but is of the world." The "boasting" or pride of life is nothing more than the selfish desire to be noticeably superior. It's the basis behind human striving, best exemplified by Vince Lombardi's statement: "Winning isn't everything—it's the only thing."

When Muhammad Ali was about to face Joe Frazier for the world heavyweight championship fight in 1971, he said, "There seems to be so much confusion. We're going to clear up this confusion on March 8. We're going to decide once and for all who is king. There's not a man alive who can whup me." Ali then jabbed the air with a half-dozen, blinding lefts. "I'm too smart," he said. Then he lifted his head and said, "I'm too pretty. I'm the king. I should be a postage stamp—that's the only way anybody can lick me."

That philosophy pulsates throughout American industry as well. Hertz boasts, "We're number one!" Avis screams out, "We try harder!" This philosophy accounts for some of the worst aspects of capitalism. Steel magnate Andrew Carnegie wrote his famous work entitled *The*

Road to Business Success to encourage aspiring young businessmen. Here's what he said:

"My advice to you, gentlemen, is to aim high. I would not give a fig to the man who does not already see himself as partner or the head of the firm. Do not rest content for a moment in your thoughts as head clerk, as foreman, or as general manager, regardless of the size of your concern, no matter how extensive. Say to yourself, 'My place is at the top.' Be king in your dreams."

Dr. Vernon C. Grounds, the former president of Denver Seminary, writes this in his book *Faith For Failure*: "Unless I am mistaken, this is the very dynamic which likewise operates in much of Christian service—the sinful desire to be noticeably superior. First, if possible. Number one. Never number two. As I see it, the church has allowed the world to impose on Christian service standards of success which are non-biblical. I am honestly afraid that American evangelicalism is guilty of idolatry. It is bowing down, if I may borrow the biting phrase from the philosopher William James, 'before the bitch goddess of success.' As disciples of Jesus Christ, too many of us are sinfully concerned about size: of sanctuaries, of salaries, of budgets, of Sunday Schools. Too many of us in God's service are sinfully preoccupied with statistics about budgets, buildings, buses, and baptisms."

Dr. Grounds is saying that as Christians our thinking needs to be in line with God's Word. In our secular colleges and universities we are teaching the world's idea of success. Unfortunately, that same philosophy is being fed to students in seminaries across the country.

REAL SUCCESS

We are called to follow in the footsteps of our Lord. And we must understand that God's standards differ radically from those of the world.

> *The Bible turns man's value system, man's idea of success, topsy-turvy. God puts on the top what fallen man has put on the bottom. Man puts on top what God says is detestable in His sight.*

In Luke 16:15, Jesus says, "What is highly esteemed among men is an abomination in the sight of God." According to Dr. Paul Reese: "If you want a picture of success, as heaven measures it, don't look for blaring bands on Broadway. Listen rather to the sound of water splashing into a basin while God incarnate, in a humility that makes angels hold their breath, sponges the grime from the feet of his undeserving disciples."

In other words, the Bible turns man's value system, man's idea of success, topsy-turvy. God puts on the top what fallen man has put on the bottom. Man puts on top what God says is detestable in His sight. God praises poverty and says to die to self.

What is dying to self? In John 12:25 Jesus says, "He who loves his life will lose it, and he who hates his life in this world will keep it for eternal life." He is telling us that one of the prerequisites for success in the eyes of God is to die to self. Our success depends upon it. Let me give you a good definition of dying to self.

When you're forgotten, neglected, or purposely set at naught, and you don't sting and hurt with the insult or the oversight, but your heart is happy being counted worthy to suffer for Jesus Christ, this is dying to self. When your good is spoken of as evil, when your wishes are crossed, and your advice disregarded, your opinions ridiculed, and you refuse to let your anger rise up in your heart, or even defend yourself, but take it in patient loving silence, this is dying to self. When you lovingly and patiently bear any disorder in your life, any irregularity, any unpunctuality, any annoyance; when you stand face to face with adversity, waste, folly, extravagance, spiritual insensibility and endure as Jesus Christ endured the cross, this is dying to self. When you are content with any food, any offering, any raiment, any society, or any interruption in your life, this is dying to self. When you never care to refer to yourself in any conversation or record your own good deeds or yearn after any commendation or desire to truly be unknown, this is dying to self. When you can see your brother prosper and have his needs met while you feel your needs are being unmet, and you can be happy with him in your spirit, this is dying to self. And when you can receive correction and reproof from one of seemingly less stature than yourself, and you can humbly submit inwardly as well as outwardly, this is dying to self.

—Author unknown

The apostle Paul warns us in 1 Corinthians 3:12 that the achievements the world apprises as gold, silver, and precious stones, God says are wood, hay, and stubble. God is warning each of us that the day is coming when every work that we do is going to be held account-able.

In Hebrews 11, we read about various men and women who were shining successes in the sight of God. This is a list of people who were in conflict with their societies. Like Jesus, Stephen, Paul, and Peter, many of them died as common criminals. None of them would be invited to speak at the prayer breakfast in Washington, D.C.

What then are God's standards for success? We know that God requires each of us to die to self. In addition, according to 1 Corinthians 13, God requires us to love one another. He tells us that He puts the highest premium on faith, hope, and love, but the greatest of these is love.

In Matthew 20:26-28 there is another criterion for success. Jesus says that whoever wants to be great must be a servant. And whoever wants to be first must be a slave, just as Christ did not come to be served but to serve and to give His life for us.

In Matthew 25:21, we see something else. Jesus stressed the importance of using God-given talents when He says, "His lord said to him, 'Well done, good and faithful servant; you were faithful over a few things, I will make you ruler over many things. Enter into the joy of your lord.' "

Whether God gives us five talents or two or even one, His criterion for success is the same—diligent faithfulness.

When we reach the end of our lives, our obituaries probably won't be in the New York Times. Our names probably will not be mentioned in the history books. But that doesn't really matter because God is going to be the final judge of our lives. Therefore, it is infinitely more important to be a follower of God's unique blueprint for our lives than it is to be a lengthy entry in the "Who's Who" of this world.

Regardless of the talent God has given us; regardless of the achievements some of us may attain in this world; we are absolutely nothing. But Jesus Christ our Lord and Savior is everything. Enabled by God's Holy Spirit and following the principles of love, service, faithfulness, and death to self, we are to be steadfast disciples of Jesus Christ. Then, no matter how the world may judge us, in the sight of God we will be truly successful.

George MacDonald has written:

> I said, let me walk in the field,
> He said, no, walk in the town.
> I said, there are no flowers there, father,
> He said, no flowers, but a crown.
>
> I said, but the skies are black,
> there is nothing but noise and din.
> And He wept as He sent me back,
> there is more my son, He said, there is sin.
>
> I said, but Father, the air is black and thick,
> and the fogs are veiling the sun.
> He answered, yet souls are sick,
> and the souls in the dark undone.

I said, I shall miss the light Father,
and friends will miss me they tell me.
He answered, choose tonight
if I am to miss you or they.

I pleaded for time to be given.
He said, it's hard to decide—
It will not seem hard in heaven
to have followed in the footsteps of your
    Guide.

I cast one look at the fields,
then I set my face to the town.
He said, my child, do you now yield?
Will you leave the flowers for the crown?

Then into his hand went mine,
and into my heart came He.
And I walk in the light divine,
the path that I had feared to see.

Walk in the path that God has set before you.
It may seem fearful, but you will achieve the
kind of success that God has designed for you.

■ GROWTH STRATEGIES ■

1. What do the following verses teach about
    being a success in God's sight?

    Matthew 20:26-28

    Matthew 25:21

    John 12:25

    1 Corinthians 13:13

2. What does our world use to measure
    success?

3. How can a person determine what his idea
    of success really is?

4. Using those tests on yourself, what is your idea of success?

5. Think of the men in your neighborhood or in your office. What are their goals?

6. What can you do to become successful in God's eyes?

CHAPTER 7

THE BALANCED LIFE

Ken Davis
Speaker, author, and entertainer

■ CHAPTER OBJECTIVE ■

My purposes in this chapter are:
(1) to define what makes a life "balanced"
(2) to discuss how to achieve a balanced life
(3) to describe briefly how we can maintain a
balanced life.

Balance is a vital part of the physical world. We see its importance in everything from car wheels to golf clubs. If a wheel is off center, the vehicle gyrates and moves awkwardly, if at all. Swing a golf club that lacks balance, and there's no telling what will happen—and that's the problem!

Since balance is so important all around us, it's logical to assume that balance is in some way important in life itself. We sense this is true even when we admit that our lives are often hopelessly out of balance.

DEFINING BALANCE

Teeter-totters in my school yard were made to carry elephants. The heavy planks attached to large pipes were more dangerous than fun. Maybe that's why we liked them so much. For little kids, though, the emphasis on sturdiness created a unique problem. Our weight was often too light to overcome the inertia of the planks. On those rare occasions when we were actually able to get the "down side" off the ground, we usually found ourselves stuck at the midway point, trapped between up and down, legs flailing in a vain attempt to get the contraption in motion again. At that moment we experienced a frustrating and terrifying version of balance. That is not what we wish to experience as Christians when we speak of the balanced life.

So, what kind of life is balanced? The balanced life is characterized by order, peace, and wholeness. This means the various parts of life are as they should be and where they should be. Each part gets the right amount of time and effort at the right time. It isn't giving each part of life the same amount of time that makes life balanced; it is giving each part the right amount of time.

> *The balanced life is characterized by order, peace, and wholeness. Each part gets the right amount of time and effort at the right time.*

Perhaps one of the best poetic descriptions of the balanced life comes from the pen of Solomon:

> *"To everything there is a season, a time for every purpose under heaven:*
>
> *A time to be born, and a time to die;*

*A time to plant, and a time to pluck
what is planted;*

A time to kill, and a time to heal;

*A time to break down, and a time to
build up;*

A time to weep, and a time to laugh;

A time to mourn, and a time to dance;

*A time to cast away stones, and a
time to gather stones;*

*A time to embrace, and a time to re-
frain from embracing;*

A time to gain, and a time to lose;

*A time to keep, and a time to throw
away;*

A time to tear, and a time to sew;

*A time to keep silence, and a time to
speak;*

A time to love, and a time to hate;

A time of war, and a time of peace"

(Eccl. 3:1-8).

Balance just for the sake of balance is not what we are talking about. You could be zero in all areas of life and be "balanced." The real challenge of the balanced life is experiencing life at its best and fullest without becoming "tilted." It is important to take an honest look at your life and ask: "Is everything where it needs to be? Am I neglecting an important area? Am I using well what God has entrusted to me?"

Our tendency is to live out of balance. When we neglect an area or overemphasize it, our lives get out of alignment. And yet we know people who try to live that way. They may spend all their time at work to the detriment of everything else. Some are socially oriented, and that becomes the focus of their lives. Others seem to live for a certain sport or hobby. In the process, these "off balance" people often lose friends, family, and even their future. Finding these descriptions all too familiar, we ask, "How do I get balance in my life?"

ACHIEVING BALANCE

When I speak to groups, some of my most effective illustrations involve the use of illusions. Magic works because we can only concentrate on one thing at a time. A magician knows that if we concentrate on what his left hand is doing, we won't even notice what his right hand does. This is also the key to making life work.

This is the place where the sharp ones usually raise their hands and ask: "If it's true that I can only concentrate on one thing at a time, aren't you admitting that it really isn't possible to live a balanced life? Balance seems to imply more than one thing."

This is a tense moment, and I naturally respond, "That's a very good question. Are there any other questions?" By the time the laughter has died down, I've had a chance to think. I try to answer in this way:

"Remember, the first word I used to define balance was 'order.' You're right, life is made up of many parts, each demanding our time and energy. Balance refers to what brings order to life. Because we can only concentrate our lives on one thing at a time, this 'thing' has to be so unique that every part of life will fall into proper order, or balance, when it is at the center."

> *No matter what particular area of life I happen to be concentrating on at the moment, I will also be concentrating on the center.*

For now, let's call this one thing around which everything else takes its proper place the organizing center of life. This organizing center has to have one essential characteristic: no matter what particular area of life I happen to be concentrating on at the moment, I will also be concentrating on the center. I know what you're thinking: "Wait a minute. Now you're telling me that I can concentrate on two things . . . just when I was beginning to agree that I could only concentrate on one thing! What do you mean?"

Good question. Are there any other questions?

Let me illustrate this truth about all of life with examples from part of life. In the area of sports, for instance, my organizing center might be to become the best football player I can be. No matter what aspect of the sport I may concentrate on (running, catching, rules, strategy, blocking), by working hard on that one thing I am actually concentrating on my organizing center for that area—to become the best football player I can be. But when I over-emphasize one part, I lose the balance provided by the organizing center. If all I do is think about strategy, I may have to change my organizing center to becoming the best coach I can be. Or, if all I do is rest, one thing is certain: my organizing center isn't what I thought it was.

Another example might be your career. You probably have a major goal you would like to achieve. Think of that as the organizing center of that part of life. The quality of your work, the reading you do, the seminars you attend, the advice you seek are all likely to relate in some way to that goal. Decisions you make and opportunities you take advantage of will in some way describe just how serious you are about the organizing center of your career.

Returning to the big picture, what then can serve as the organizing center for all of life? Something capable of filling that complicated purpose. Something by which everything else in life can be evaluated, organized, and balanced. Something that gives importance and value to whatever good thing we do. Finding that one thing and making it the organizing center of life will bring balance.

It isn't surprising to discover that Jesus was asked this same "'You shall love the Lord your God with all your heart, with all your soul, and mind.' This is the first and great commandment. And the second is like it: 'You shall love your neighbor as yourself.' On these two commandments hang all the Law and the Prophets" (Matt. 22:37-40).

Notice how Jesus concluded His response. His words could be paraphrased: "Concentrate on this, and you will find everything else taking its proper place."

Jesus defines the center of life and what immediately surrounds it. The organizing center is, "Love God with all your heart, soul, and mind." What surrounds it—the way it affects our lives—is, "Love your neighbor as yourself."

Every chapter in this book is about the balanced life. Each author views his reader as a person who has allowed God to become the organizing center, the Master, of life. If this has been a recent event for you, that is, you have recently accepted Christ as your Savior, much of the difficulty or delight you may be experiencing can be explained as God's presence shifting parts of your life so that they approach the point of balance. The changes are not always easy, or easy to understand.

These chapters attempt to help you cooperate with what God is already trying to create in you. Remember, if you have invited Christ to take over the central place in your life, you already have the most important component of a balanced life. When Jesus crossed the doorway of your life He made this announcement: "I have come that they may have life, and that they may have it more abundantly" (John 10:10).

MAINTAINING BALANCE

If a specific area of your life is out of balance, you should be able to find help to get it back in balance in one of the chapters in this book. You also will be presented with challenges and questions to help you expand the balance of your life. You may find out that God has some new priorities for you!

When faced with several out-of-balance areas, remind yourself, "I can only concentrate on one thing at a time." You'll eventually want to do something about every area, but for now ask God to help you choose an area of your life that you can definitely move toward balance. It may be something as simple yet challenging as planning how to demonstrate love to each member of your family before this day is over.

Use the table of contents of this book to keep a "balance inventory." Make a note on your weekly or monthly calendar to spend a few minutes reviewing the areas covered while asking: "Are my actions in this area moving me toward or away from balance and order?"

If you are a recent believer, you will be amazed at all that is involved in a healthy spiritual life. Like a sudden shifted weight on a teeter-totter, you may even feel as if your life is in danger of losing balance. When you feel like this remember the shortest, most sincere prayer in the Bible: "Help!" (Matt. 14:30). Peter had just experienced the exhilaration of walking by faith on water. He suddenly realized what was happening. He was doing something beyond himself. At that moment, he stopped concentrating on who was making this happen and shifted his concentration to what was happening. He started to sink like a stone. (Maybe that's when Jesus decided to nickname him "Rocky.") Your adventure in the balanced Christian life is as real and potentially unnerving as Peter's walk on the waves. The occasional sensation of sinking should remind you to ask Christ for help.

A young Christian leader was given this direction: "Meditate on these things; give yourself entirely to them, that your progress may be evident to all" (1 Tim. 4:15). Remember, on this side of eternity, God expects progress more than perfection.

There are four areas in which God has consistently challenged me toward balance: taking time to grow in my faith; spending time with my family; demonstrating excellence in my work; and taking time for myself. I have found these areas to be challenges for many of the men I meet during my speaking opportunities. Each of these is ably covered in other chapters, so I will just touch on them briefly.

Take Time to Grow in Your Faith

Growing in faith is a matter of knowledge and action. The knowledge part is the simple step; doing what needs to be done takes a lifetime. You'll never "find the time," and it won't just happen. The time will have to be taken, planned, and scheduled. It will take time to let God talk to you through His Word, to speak to Him in prayer, to learn from and worship with other Christians.

Spend Time with Your Family

Until recently, I was one of those men who spoke of "quality time" with my wife and children when I couldn't have "quantity time." Then a wise and loving older Christian asked me, "Do you really think your kids can tell the difference?" It occurred to me that I was the

only one determining how much time I spent
with my family. So I began to think more
about their needs than my schedule.

A recent survey showed that dads spend less
than fifteen minutes a week with their children. The only way I was able to change that
statistic in my life was to take the time to play
and talk with them, finding out about school
and letting them know a little about what happens in my life, including how I sense God is
working. I've realized that family members are
the people most directly affected by my decision to make Jesus Christ the organizing center of my life. If my life isn't balanced, they'll
know it.

My kids have a game called Nintendo. I hate
the game. It usually drives me nuts, because
I'm no good at it. But my younger daughter
loves playing this game, and she takes delight
in beating me. She laughs like crazy at my in-
eptness and never fails to wonder out loud if
I'll ever be able to get beyond the first screen.
There's nothing "spiritual" about this activity.
But I've found that if I affirm what is important to my children, they are much more likely
to seriously consider what is important to me.

This same pattern is even more important to
practice with my wife. My children will be out
on their own soon, but my wife and I will
spend the rest of our lives together. This
means that keeping our relationship healthy is
a big part of keeping my life in balance. There
is a small but extremely romantic difference between telling your wife you want to spend
some time doing what she would like to do,
and being subtle and sneaky enough to discover what that is and planning to do it. The

first time I ever pulled off the road in front of
an antique sign without being asked, I knew I
was on to something. Unlike my children, my
wife doesn't laugh at me when I do things like
that . . . but wonderful things do happen!

If you are a new Christian, your actions may
at first seem strange to your family. But they
will be more likely to follow your lead if they
see your honest attempts to make God the organizing center of your life. You might start by
making this sort of announcement before the
next family meal: "Before we eat, I'd like to say
two things. First, thank you, (wife), for prepar-
ing this food for us. I know I don't appreciate
all you do for us as much as I should. Second,
I'm discovering God in a way that is new for
me. One thing I've learned is that whatever we
have to wear, use, spend, or eat really comes
from Him. So, I'd like to say thank you to Him
in prayer. 'Thank You, God, for this food!'"

Demonstrate Excellence in Your Work

I am constantly challenged to keep work in balance. Because of the amount of time it consumes, work tends to drift to the center. But
it's more than that. I have a tendency to feel
that unless I'm really successful in my work
and bringing home the big paycheck, my family will fall apart. But that's a myth. Struggling together is better than succeeding apart.
I have talked with many successful people who
have drifted away from their families. They
look back to the struggling years with fond-
ness, because they faced things together then;
they had something in common.

Although work is not the most important part
of life, I want to emphasize that how we do the

work is very important. Strive for excellence. Don't try to get by with less. Don't slough off. Don't ignore your responsibilities. One of the best ways to make your faith ring true to your fellow workers is by your commitment to excellence and honesty—excellence in the quality of your work and in the quality of your life at work.

I have a friend who just sold a very large business to one of the top corporations in the country. He had difficulty finding the right buyer. He probably could have sold it long ago, but he insisted that whoever became the new owner would have to commit to taking care of the people who had worked for him all those years. No one wanted to promise that. The excellence in his life was clear because he refused to sell to anyone who was going to drop the hundreds of faithful employees to whom he was committed. He showed me that integrity and excellence can be the flavor of a balanced life.

> *Strive for excellence. Don't try to get by with less. Don't slough off. Don't ignore your responsibilities. One of the best ways to make your faith ring true to your fellow workers is by your commitment to excellence and honesty.*

Take Time for Yourself

Remember that Jesus' description of the center of life did not eliminate personal time. The first task beyond loving God, He said, was loving those around us as ourselves. How you treat yourself will directly affect how you treat others . (And even how long you are around to treat them.)

The two most common evidences of self-neglect are fatigue and apathy. The other day I heard someone say (and it hit me right between the eyes) that one of Satan's most effective ploys is to get a man completely worn out. When we are overextended we begin to make choices based on urgency rather than priority. Crucial things like rest, proper nutrition, and exercise are put on hold. This kind of decision-making works well for a while, but eventually we discover we are running on empty.

Apathy, on the other hand, can be a problem whether we're tired or not. Apathy reflects a decision to stop growing in certain areas of life. Someone has said that when you stop growing, you start dying. This applies to the mind. This doesn't just mean learning work-related knowledge. Read and learn broadly. Don't get trapped into being an "expert" in one tiny corner of the universe.

The greatest model of the balanced life, lived out by Jesus Christ, involved this pattern of constant growth. Luke 2:52 says, "And Jesus increased in wisdom and stature, and in favor with God and men" (Luke 2:52). I encourage you to keep growing in every way. Working through this book will give you a good start!

These brief lessons have cost me, but it has been worth it. Some mistakes still haunt me. I almost lost my family by working over three hundred days a year. I'm grateful that God intervened and turned me around. Like the sun, He keeps my planets in order. He creates and helps maintain balance.

If you want a balanced life, live it with God at the center.

■ GROWTH STRATEGIES ■

1.   What can we learn from these verses
     about developing all areas of life?

     Ecclesiastes 3:1-8

     Matthew 6:24

     Luke 2:52

     John 10:10

     Romans 12:1-2

     1 Corinthians 6:19-20

2. What should be the organizing center of
    life? (Matt. 22:37-40.)

3. Which of these areas consumes most of
    your time?

    ☐ Growing in your faith?

    ☐ Being with your family?

    ☐ Demonstrating excellence at work?

    ☐ Taking time for yourself?

4. Which area receives the least amount of
    your time and attention?

5. What is the organizing center of your life?
    What would you like it to be?

6. What changes could you make to live a balanced life, centering it around Christ?

TIME AND MONEY

For most Christians, maintaining their sense of balance is dependent on their understanding and control of time and money. Our date books and check books are two of the strongest pieces of evidence in determining the degree of balance in our lives. The first is a constant for everyone—twenty-four hours each day. The second varies greatly. Both are God-given resources.

Most of us decide how we spend the majority of our time. Even the time commitments that we call "out of our control" are usually the result of decisions we've made. For instance, few men make this conscious decision: "From this day forward my life will revolve around my work, or my sport, or my hobby." But daily decisions, lived into habits, add up to that big decision. There is real change involved in even considering reordering long-established patterns.

If God's name is on the door of the central office of our lives, what voice does He have in the allocation of those resources of time and money?

CHAPTER 8

LIVING WITHIN LIMITS

Dr. Howard Edington
Pastor, First Presbyterian Church,
Orlando, Florida

■ CHAPTER OBJECTIVE ■

Understanding what it means to be disciplined
is essential to understanding what it means to
live within limits.

The critical issue for Christians today is to live disciplined lives. The word discipline has fallen into disfavor in a permissive society where people are unwilling to deny themselves anything. But that in no way alters its importance. Understanding what it means to be disciplined is essential to understanding what it means to live within limits.

DISCIPLINED RELATIONSHIPS

Discipline, or lack of it, affects all areas of life. Perhaps this is most clearly seen in our relationships. Life is built on a set of basic areas of trust. When you take your car to the service station and tell them to fix the carburetor, you trust that they are going to do what you ask, do it properly, and not charge more than is reasonable.

That sense of trust is part of all human relationships: business partnerships must be based on trust. Once trust is broken, the whole partnership comes unglued. The same is true of marriage. I trust my wife to be faithful to the vows she spoke at our wedding, and she has the right to trust that I will be faithful to those same vows.

Building and maintaining trust involves discipline. We have to resist the temptation to pursue our selfish desires and, instead, pursue whatever fosters, encourages, and maintains a sense of trust between ourselves and others.

DISCIPLINED CONVERSATION

I had a conversation at a restaurant with a man who is a believer and very sincere in his faith, as far as I can determine. Yet his language was straight from the gutter. He knew I was a minister, but that didn't slow him down.

I think people (men especially) use bad language for one of three reasons:

1. Some men think it makes them macho. They may feel, consciously or unconsciously, that the only way they can assert their manhood is to use this kind of language. But it is simply a cover for insecurity and low self-esteem.

2. Some men think it's sophisticated. Hollywood puts "R" ratings on movies because they want to reach the sophisticated public. To obtain an "R" rating, filmmakers sprinkle gratuitous profanity throughout the film. It has little or nothing to do with the story line—it is put there just to achieve the rating. But I've never heard anyone spew out

obscenities and look and sound sophisticated at the same time.

3.   Some men are incapable of expressing strong feelings without using profanity. The man with whom I spoke at the restaurant had strong feelings, but he could not articulate them in decent language. He had formed the habit of equating emotion, particularly anger, with profanity.

We need to discipline our tongues to use language that is constructive and healthy and to avoid using the name of God in any way that diminishes His holiness.

DISCIPLINED COMMITMENTS

I constantly see people in the church who get completely burned out physically, emotionally, and spiritually because they can't say no. They think that the way to express their faith is to work themselves into the ground. But the disciplined Christian life means that you exercise balance and moderation. Christian work should not drain away the time you need to develop your personal relationship with God, including the disciplines of silence and prayer. Those disciplines are critical to the development of your Christian life.

> *If you engage in frenetic activity, and you can't say no to anything or anybody, you will very quickly stunt your intimacy with the Lord.*

On the night the Titanic sank, the wildly celebrating passengers jammed the ship's radio, sending silly, senseless messages to friends and relatives back home. Other ships in the area could not get through with radio warnings of the presence of icebergs. This is a picture of our lives: sometimes we are so jammed with silly, senseless activities that the saving Word of God cannot get through to us. We find ourselves so busy doing "church work" that we miss out on doing the true work of the Church. If you engage in frenetic activity, and you can't say no to anything or anybody, you will very quickly stunt your intimacy with the Lord.

Jesus ministered out of power, not out of guilt. Thousands of people knew Jesus and knew that He was the answer to their questions, problems, and difficulties in life. And yet, while on earth, Jesus touched only a small percentage of the people who were in need. This is a beautiful expression of the fact that Jesus was both divine and human. He had the divine power to heal physically, spiritually, mentally, and emotionally. But He was not unlimited in His energy; He needed rest.

At one point, Jesus was so exhausted that He fell asleep in a boat on the Sea of Galilee in the middle of a storm. At times, Jesus took Himself away from the press of the crowds and His responsibilities to spend time alone with the Father. When Jesus did that, He always left behind people who had profound needs. However, when He returned, people were drawn to Him as never before. I believe it was because of His time away. The discipline of renewal and refreshment so recharged Jesus spiritually that when He returned, the power of God literally radiated from Him and drew people like iron to a magnet.

One of the great passages in the New Testament is Matthew 9 where Jesus pulls His disciples aside and says, "The harvest truly is plentiful, but the laborers are few" (v. 37). In essence Jesus is saying, "I cannot cover it all. I am divine, but I am also human. I need your help. I am going to charge you with power, and I want you to go out and to minister in My name. And here is how I want you to do it." Then Jesus delivers this wonderful set of instructions, phrase by phrase: "Travel light; be careful with whom you associate; when you go into a house, deliver the blessing of God upon that house; if you encounter a person or group unwilling to hear what you have to say, shake the dust off your feet and get on to something else; when you get into trouble, do not worry because I am going to be there with you; when you are forced to speak, do not worry about what to say because God will give you the words; preach that the kingdom of heaven is at hand" (see Matt. 10). There is an urgency to all this. Jesus gives the disciples this great set of instructions. He says, in effect, "You go do the work."

Later in the Gospels it says that the disciples were so excited they said, "Lord, you should have seen what happened!" Jesus answered, "I did see—I saw that in what you were doing, Satan was being battered, the angels were singing in heaven, and there was a great celebration" (see Luke 10:17-24).

Jesus had power limited by His humanity. His power to touch human need is multiplied by investing that power in us, so that we become the agents of the gospel.

LIMITATIONS AND WEAKNESSES

One of the most difficult aspects of personal discipline is understanding our limitations and weaknesses. It helps to have an individual (or a group) who can clarify those for us.

I am blessed with a wife who is my biggest fan and my best critic. To have someone who loves you unconditionally, a spouse or a good friend, is a blessing beyond description, especially when that person (in the context of a loving relationship) is also able to address your weaknesses. He or she will do it in such a way that ego does not confuse the issue.

It is also crucial to have this type of relationship with a group of believers. That is why it is incredibly important for us to build covenant relationships with a small group of Christians. A covenant group fulfills such a role. It is a committed group whose primary responsibility is to hold one another accountable and to help each other become men of God—all that He created them to be. These relationships provide unconditional love and faithfulness.

Problems develop when someone analyzes our weaknesses and gives us "constructive criticism" without loving us. Then we become wounded and we strike back. In the process, our weakness never gets addressed or strengthened.

> *The Christian life was never meant to be lived in isolation. We need each other.*

CONSUMPTION AND ACQUISITION

Conspicuous consumption has become almost synonymous with America. Just about every aspect of our society is designed to encourage it. When Thomas Jefferson spoke of the pursuit of happiness, that was the last thing he had in mind.

I do not think it is a sin to be rich; I do not find that stated anywhere in the Bible. But what we do with our riches can be sinful. The more we acquire and the more affluent we become, the more difficult it is for us to depend on God. When we begin to feel, "I have it made," or "I am a self-made person," we sever the nerve of our relationship with God. No matter how good or how bad life was, Jesus never lost His sense of total dependence upon God. That is what enabled Him to keep a proper perspective on life and the "things" of life.

When Trish and I were married almost twenty-five years ago, one of our friends gave us a beautiful Lalique crystal vase. It has a place of honor in our living room. It is valuable, and we love it. We do not love it because it is valuable, but because our friend gave it to us and because we have had it for twenty-five years.

Not long ago, we were invited to a palatial home here in Orlando. It was an absolutely incredible place. We stepped through the front door. In the enormous foyer was a huge table. On that table was every piece of Lalique crystal ever made. I was astonished, and I began to think about how much it cost. Then I remembered the vase that sits in our living room, and I realized that when you have them all, not one of them has any particular value. If you build that in to your life as an operating principle, then you will acquire things in a more disciplined manner.

The discipline of "responsible affluence" is almost a contradiction in terms. But it is possible to achieve. We must be disciplined in how we spend money.

DISCIPLINED POWER

Second Timothy 1:7 says, "For God has not given us a spirit of fear, but of power and of love and of a sound mind." Power comes out of discipline. A wild horse possesses uncontrolled and destructive power. But when the horse is broken and harnessed, its power is not diminished but is directed and channeled. Paul is saying that a life harnessed to the great, glorious truths of Christianity means a life of freedom, not a life of slavery. It means a life of joy, not drudgery. Discipline in the Christian experience is joyous, not restraining and constraining. When you engage in discipline, in essence you establish and enhance your relationship to God so that His power flows through you.

If you want to achieve physical strength and power, the only way to do it is to engage in the discipline of physical training—jogging, cardiovascular exercises, lifting weights, and using Nautilus machines. It's not going to happen any other way. Out of the discipline of physical training comes physical strength and power.

The same is true spiritually. We must discipline ourselves to study the Word, to pray, to love others, and to be good stewards of our resources.

PRACTICING THE PRESENCE

I am much influenced by Brother Lawrence's concept of practicing the presence of Jesus. It is critical for us to engage in the daily discipline of practicing the presence of Christ in our lives. Every day I make myself aware of the fact that Jesus is with me every single moment by having an extra chair in my office. That chair is His; nobody else sits in it. If I have a meeting involving eight people, then I bring in an extra chair. It is a visual reminder of a spiritual reality.

I spend a lot of time driving back and forth to the church, to the hospital, or to wherever my work takes me, and I get caught in traffic. I try to use that time to speak to Jesus as though He is sitting in the front seat with me. People sitting behind me at the stoplight may wonder what is going on, but that's okay. Henry Ford said, "Your best friend is the person who draws the best out of you." Jesus draws the best out of me. Whatever good is there, He draws it out. He is my best friend, so I talk to Him like that. It is not a formalized prayer, not something that anybody would want to put into print. I just talk to Him. As I walk down the hospital corridors on my way to minister to someone, I sense that Christ is walking at my side, and I ask Him to help me say and do the right things. The more I sense His presence, the more I experience His power.

> *Out of the discipline comes the power. If you engage in the discipline of practicing the presence of Jesus in your life, you will begin to tap into this awesome spiritual power yourself.*

Spirituality is not automatic. It takes submission, obedience, and discipline. If you are going to be spiritually fit, you have to work at it.

■ GROWTH STRATEGIES ■

1. What do these passages teach about personal discipline?

   Proverbs 12:11

   Ecclesiastes 3:1-8

   Luke 12:35-48

   John 9:4

   1 Corinthians 9:27

   2 Timothy 1:7

2. What evidence of undisciplined lives do you see in the world?

3. In which of the following areas are you most disciplined: relationships, communication/ language, commitments, possessions/ money, spiritual life?

4. In which area are you the least disciplined?

5. What could you do to become more disciplined in that area?

6. What should be your first step to begin "practicing the presence of Christ"?

Personal and Progressive Commitment in Your Relationships with Others

CHAPTER 9

MARRIAGE/SPOUSE

Pat Williams
General Manager,
Orlando Magic Professional Basketball Team

■ CHAPTER OBJECTIVE ■

"What is my responsibility in my marriage?"
"What does it take to build a good marriage?"
"How can I encourage my wife?" This chapter
will explain how your faith in Christ should af-
fect your marriage.

GOD'S EXPECTATIONS

Ephesians 5:25 says that husbands are to love
their wives "as Christ loved the church." Even
though my eyes passed over those words for
years, like many Christian husbands, I kind of
ignored it. I would jump over it because it
seemed impossible. Christ loved the church to
the point that He gave His life. That's hard —
it's nigh onto impossible. But that's God's blueprint for men and how they are to relate to
their wives. It's tough, and it's extremely
stretching and challenging, but that's the command we have been given.

A CONTINUAL PROCESS

That should be our goal — to love our wives as
Christ loved the church. That involves action,

and it's a *daily* issue. You never reach the point where it's all over and you're finished. I don't think you can love your wife like Christ loved the church on Monday and expect that love to last for a week or a month.

Jill often reminds me that there is no such thing in marriage as stacking up points from yesterday. We kid each other about this, but "What have you done for me lately?" seems to be the approach that has to be taken. It has to be a daily issue with no dwelling on the past because the past doesn't count. Obviously you have to build on a foundation, but you also have to love her every day.

When Jill and I wrote *Rekindled*, we enjoyed telling how we had rediscovered love in our marriage. Even though that book was a milestone for us, we can't now relax and take our relationship for granted.

Even now, in a weak moment, Jill will say, "You know you've helped write this great book, datatatada! Now you think your part is done — you've gone to sleep on me." That is a very frank reminder that men must pay attention to this every day, because a marriage *can* just drift apart.

"Drifting" is the key word. Usually we don't decide to move apart, we just slowly drift into trouble.

BUSY-NESS

Men often get totally preoccupied with their work, and women perhaps in their extracurricular activities or their careers. Then the little things it takes to have a good marriage begin

to be ignored. After a while, there is an awareness that the relationship is losing its excitement. It's very insidious. Many people believe
that everything goes along fine in a marriage
until there is a huge explosion and the whole
thing bombs out in one day. But it doesn't happen that way. Instead, marriages erode gradually.

> *"Drifting" is the key word. Usually
> we don't decide to move apart, we
> just slowly drift into trouble.*

WAKE UP!

Although both the husband and the wife share
the responsibility for making a marriage work,
men must wake up! Most women are waiting
for their men to become as interested and en-
thusiastic about the marriage as they are
about golf or fishing or work. Men need to
make a total commitment to this relationship
and get fired up about their homes and their
marriages. I think many wives would say that
their marriages are boring because the men
don't have much enthusiasm for them.

I know this sounds unfair — like I'm placing
all the blame and responsibility on husbands,
but I really am convinced that the men are the
ones who need to make the turn. Most wives
are just waiting, sitting there just pleading for
the husband to care, to get involved.

In our situation, the marriage wasn't bad. I
didn't think it was bad. But Jill knew that

there had to be more to it. And she wasn't experiencing that.

> *Women see it differently. For them,*
> *marriage can be like baking*
> *a pie. They want to enjoy it*
> *and share it with others.*

LOVE IS A VERB

Often people say, "I just don't have any feelings, loving feelings, anymore." I really am convinced that loving actions create the loving feelings. In other words, if we act as if we are in love, the loving feelings will flow from the loving actions. You shouldn't wait for a warm, gooey, loving feeling to take over and then jump into action. So many people seem to think that that's what is going to happen, but it doesn't work that way.

Love is an action — it means doing, serving, giving. There are dozens of acts of love that can be done on a daily basis, everything from setting the table to just listening. I find that as a man begins to demonstrate Christ-like love toward his wife, she usually cannot resist a response. At first she may feel nothing, and she may be emotionally burned out, but most wives cannot help but respond to a husband who demonstrates his love for her in tangible ways.

PERSISTENCE

You've got to stay with it. As I look back on our experience, the one thing that I did possess when the marriage came crashing down was persistence. I took a bulldog type of approach — hang on and keep at it. Persistence means that you have to be totally committed to this issue.

Remember your wedding vows? That's what you promised — to hang on and hang together until death. Today the attitude seems to be (even in Christian homes) that we can always get out of this marriage. But divorce should not be an option. Divorce should be totally locked away and out of the question or the marriage will be in trouble. That's commitment.

Persistence and commitment also relate to Ephesians 5:25. Christ loved the church through many sins and many rejections. Christ loves us unconditionally. That command of Ephesians 5:25 is just overwhelming. It says "Husbands love your wives...." Nowhere in Scripture does it say "Wives love your husbands." God knows that wives will love if they are loved.

INITIATORS

Women are responders, and so men need to be initiators. In so many cases, however, women are not living with men who take the initiative. When the wife has to be the initiator, her whole life gets out of whack because she was made to respond not to initiate.

Some men are afraid to initiate because they live with a fear of rejection. Others don't work at their marriages because life at home and life in the family is not all that exciting or fun. There's a lot of hard work and few "perks" or "payoffs." It seems more exciting at their offices, on golfing weekends, on fishing trips, at ball games, and even watching television. Life at home with the family slides way down the list of interesting and exciting things to do. That's one of the lies our society feeds us...that everything we do should be fun, interesting, and exciting. If it's boring, we don't want to spend time doing it.

Family life can be boring and routine, but it doesn't have to be. It forms the foundation of our lives and of society. Marriage and family are God's ideas, his plans for life. Men have got to reprioritize and understand that God is a whole lot more concerned with their families and their marriages than He is with their golf game or their business success or how many fish they caught or how many games they watched on TV.

HARD WORK

The fact is that building a good marriage is hard work. It must be a total commitment that involves every waking moment. This includes thinking, planning, and paying attention to details. Being a good husband and a good father can be very time consuming. It's a huge job.

BALANCE AND BUSINESS

At this point you may be saying, "With all the demands of work and home, how can a person fit it all in?" That's a good question, and the same answers you find at work are valid at home — time management and delegation.

That has helped me more than anything, especially now that our children are older. Their activities are increasing dramatically and the time demands on us with our children are enormous right now. Our days start really early, and there is no time to waste. Right now I'm locked into my marriage, the children, my work, and our ministry. I have to be very careful that Jill and I get enough time alone. Whether it's breakfast, a walk around the neighborhood, a dinner date, or whatever, she has to get that time.

In all of my busy-ness, Jill has to be a priority. I've got to make that happen every week or we're going to get into serious trouble again.

Time management means putting special times together in the schedule book, like an important business appointment. There should also be spontaneous events. These could include meeting downtown for lunch together, surprising her with concert tickets (and a babysitter), or an escape weekend.

Men often think of their lives as jigsaw puzzles. You put the whole puzzle of your life together, and as you put the pieces in, you don't go back and redo them. One of the pieces is your marriage and your family.

> *The world is going to do everything it can to snuff your marriage out.*

After that is in place, you can get on with the other parts of life that are not in place.

Women see it differently. For them, marriage can be like baking a pie. They want to enjoy it and share it with others. Out of marriage they want romance, surprises, creativity, fun, adventure, and excitement. With all the other demands of life, that's hard work. It's hard work to be romantic and creative.

RELATING TO AN "UNBELIEVING" WIFE

If your wife does not share your commitment to Christ, you have to be very sensitive to her. Don't try to force your faith on her and expect her to change. It may be a very long process. You must remain committed to the marriage, even though now you are "unequally yoked" (2 Corinthians 6:14). Your one great mission is to lead her to Christ. But this must be done with great wisdom and care or you will drive her further away. Often God will use the Christian mate to lead his or her partner to the Lord.

More common are marriages where there has been a mutual commitment to Christ, but both partners have gotten out of touch with the Lord and have turned from Him totally. Then their marriage goes down the tubes. Suddenly, one of the partners is brought back to the Lord, and the other partner is still out there spiritually dead. I'm convinced that most of the problems in marriage are spiritual. And the fact that both people are Christians is no guarantee that the marriage is going to be good. It certainly helps, and it gives you a base on which to work. But no matter how strong you are spiritually now, unless it's dealt with on a daily basis, the marriage can get in serious trouble.

The most effective way to win a spouse to the Lord is through your life; living and loving for Christ. Your new faith should improve your relationships at home. And, hopefully, your wife will be drawn to Christ. Of course you should be ready to share your faith when the opportunity arises (1 Peter 3:15).

ENCOURAGING A SPOUSE TO GROW

Even in our tough times I was always pretty good at this. Jill is very talented and I've always encouraged her to stretch herself in all areas. Jill doesn't have a lot of confidence in herself, but she's amazingly versatile. She's an artist and a photographer. She has musical skills, and she has just received her real estate license. She can write...and on and on. She's amazing. I have always pushed her to develop those skills to the utmost.

I've noticed, however, that there are many men who feel threatened when their wives do anything other than sit at home. But I believe that the husband's responsibility as the head of the house is to create an atmosphere that will allow his wife and children to live up to 100% of their maximum potential. It's unbelievable the number of women who feel stifled and frustrated because they cannot live to their potential. Their husbands hold them back, perhaps because they're fearful that their wives will outdo them or make them look bad, or that she'll run off with somebody else.

I don't know. But there's a terrific problem in this area.

Husbands should encourage and "push" their wives in a loving and sensitive manner. It can't be done in a dictatorial way. Again, this comes from knowing your mate, and really studying her. Jill has an interest in doing all these things and my job is to be there and encourage her and be her cheerleader. If I sense that she has no interest and just hates to do something, then hopefully I'm wise enough to say "forget it."

It's that way with kids and their activities too. We have exposed ours to just about everything — sports, music, art, acting, etc. We're learning that when a child just absolutely hates to go, or just doesn't want to be there, that's a pretty good indication the activity is not his hot button. If he's just ecstatic about going to swimming every day but can't stand going to art class, hates it, and cries when you drop him off, then forget art class and focus on the swimming.

COMMUNICATION

Communication is at the heart of any good relationship. There are two kinds of communication: "chatter" and deep communication.

Chatter is the kind of talk that happens spontaneously throughout the day. You talk about the kids, the schedule, the weather, the house. It happens over dinner, after work, on the phone...whenever you're together. Chatter is important. Don't be the silent type who plops down in the chair after work and hides behind the paper.

But there must also be times of deep communication. These are those serious and private times when you talk about your feelings, your marriage, your faith, your future, your dreams, your budget, and your children. These times have to be a priority. Serious talk can very easily get crowded out. The world is not out to give you a good marriage. In fact, the world is going to do everything it can to snuff your marriage out. And so you have to learn to keep the world at arm's length and make communication the highest of priorities.

Sometimes you have to say "no." Pat Morley says that in making a decision about how to spend your time, ask: "Who will be crying at my funeral?" In other words if the choice is speaking to a Kiwanis meeting on Thursday night or being at your son's Little League game, which of the two groups will be crying at your funeral? That helps put things back into perspective.

FINDING HELP

Asking for help can be such an embarrassment, but often it's necessary. That was my problem when my marriage came tumbling down in December of '82. I was so embarrassed. I really didn't know where to turn, and I considered checking with some of my Christian leadership friends, but I could not do it. I was just absolutely mortified... ashamed...embarrassed. I couldn't do it.

Fortunately I read *Love Life* by Dr. Ed Wheat. That turned out to be my marriage counselor.

If you know of a trained professional who is coming from the proper spiritual perspective,

go to him or her and get some help. I still recommend *Love Life*. I believe it is the finest ma-
terial ever prepared on how to build intimacy
and love and how to rekindle love in any marriage.

> *Most men I know won't even ask*
> *for directions when they are lost*
> *on the highway.*

Pride is the real reason men won't seek help.
Most men I know won't even ask for directions
when they are lost on the highway. We think,
I can handle this. We're so proud, we're so self-
sufficient, and just like John Wayne, we don't
want to talk about our needs. "Real men don't
eat quiche," and they don't admit their needs.

Sometimes it takes an absolute crisis for God
to do a mighty work. He must take an impossible man and crush him, because until a man
gets absolutely crushed, he's not even interested in responding. But once God crushes
him, the guy is like a whipped puppy. At that
point, he will do whatever it takes to make his
marriage right. But often it takes the crisis
and the absolute disaster to get the man hum-
bled to the point that he will pay attention. It
took that for God to make me listen.

A wise friend can be a valuable counselor. If
you know someone who has your best interest
at heart, is a good listener, and has wisdom, go
to him. If you don't have a friend like that,
seek an outside counselor. But don't go blab-

bing your story around the world. That will cause you far more trouble in the long run.

Husbands, love your wives as Christ loved the church.

■ GROWTH STRATEGIES ■

1. What do these passages teach about marriage?

   Proverbs 5:15-23

   1 Corinthians 13

   Ephesians 5:25, 33

   Colossians 3:19

   James 4:1-3

2. In what areas of your marriage are you drifting apart from your wife?

3. What steps can you take to make your marriage more interesting? How can you initiate those changes?

4. What is the connection between loving feelings and loving actions?

5. What can you do to make your wife part of your weekly schedule?

6. How can you help your wife develop as a person, grow spiritually, and reach her potential?

CHAPTER 10

FAMILY/CHILDREN

Bill Glass
Bill Glass Evangelistic Association

■ CHAPTER OBJECTIVE ■

To encourage men to give and receive "The Blessing."

THE BIBLE AND THE FAMILY

The Bible says a great deal about the family. From the very beginning, the relationship between parents and their children was of paramount importance. This is evident in the verbal blessing that was passed from generation to generation.

Both Esau and Jacob were intensely interested in getting this blessing from their father. In Genesis 27 we read about Esau weeping and pleading for the blessing that the father had inadvertently given to Jacob. Esau was so upset over it that he said, "Jacob has cheated me out of two things, my birthright and my blessing." But he was more upset over losing the blessing than he was over losing the birthright. The birthright involved the financial inheritance; the blessing was simply a formality. I was puzzled that Esau was more upset about losing the blessing than he was the birthright until I worked with people who had ruined their lives after missing the blessing.

I work in prisons a great deal. In my prison work I run into men and women who did not receive the blessing from their parents. This contributed to their choice to follow a life of crime. There is something about not getting the father's blessing that makes a man dangerous. The reason I mention father is that most of the time a mother will give her blessing, but a father, for some reason, doesn't know how. Perhaps it's because he is so determined to be the tough, macho man that he neglects to bless his sons and daughters. That's always a mistake. Of course there are mothers who make the same mistake, but fathers tend to do it more often.

Blessing means "well-words." It is speaking positive, affirming, and healing words to someone—words that cause a person to feel well, accepted, and acceptable. I've been preaching about the blessing for many years, because I've seen what the lack of it produces in prisons. My message is that one of the missing ingredients in the American family is this lack of blessing . . . particularly by the father.

The blessing is not something that is given just once. It should be given continually. Words meant much more to the ancient Jew than they do today. To the Jew, a word spoken was like an arrow that went out and was irretrievable. You could never take it back.

> *A parent should love his child the way God loves us. God says, "I love you regardless of what you do." It's an unconditional love.*

The blessing referred to in Genesis 27 was this kind. It was given one time to the elder son. It was a formal acknowledgment of that son's birthright. But in modern times, a blessing is not given only in a formal sense; it is something that should be given equally to every child on a regular basis.

As the child grows, parents should discipline the child's negative, irresponsible actions and bless the positive behavior. They should also bless the child's unique personality—who he or she is—not just praise positive behavior.

Actually, this mirrors God's love. A parent should love his child the way God loves us. God says, "I love you regardless of what you do." It's an unconditional love. If you say, "I love you because you do thus and so," you are making your love conditional. The reverse implication is "If you don't do thus and so, then I won't love you." Your children should realize that you love them for who they are.

THE REBEL

Sometimes you must make a special effort toward the son or daughter who strays, just as Jesus left the ninety-nine sheep to go after the one lost sheep. Often the ones left behind misunderstand why you go after the one, and they don't like it. One father was told by his son, "I have never been involved in a life of corruption as my younger brother has, and yet you seem to favor him over me!"

Of course that's not true. You go after the one to retrieve him from harm because you love him. This type of situation demands some skill on the part of the father. If one son or daughter is a committed Christian and has lived a good, clean life, and the other one has lived a life of debauchery, you must communicate love equally to both based on who they are, not on what they have or haven't done.

LOVE IS SPELLED T-I-M-E

One of the ways to spell love is by spending quantity and quality time with our children. If I say I spend "quality" time with my child, even though I can't give him "quantity" time, I am rationalizing. It has to be both.

Some parents give their children a tremendous quantity of time, but they don't bless them. I've heard mothers talk to their children and I'm horrified by their criticism of the child's every move. "Don't put your hand in your mouth; don't look at that; don't do this; do this; do the other thing!" The child is harassed by the mother. Sometimes I just want to yell, "Shut up and give the kid a break!" That child is getting an intense amount of quantity time. But it's a negative kind of attention.

DISCIPLINE

Quality time includes discipline as well as blessing. Just as we affirm a child for positive behavior, discipline involves punishing a child for negative behavior. In other words, children need to be spanked when they act badly or persist in wanting their own way. Use something that only stings but doesn't bruise. Scripture says that if we "spare the rod" we will spoil the child (Prov. 13:24).

Be careful to let a child know that your love does not depend on his or her successes. You need to separate the disciplinary action from your love. Tell him or her, "I love you, and I think you're great, but what you did wasn't like you. What you did was wrong. So I'm punishing you for that bad act, not for who you are as a person."

As children get older, you should move away from spanking altogether. In the early teens, remove privileges. By the time they are in their late teens, they probably don't need punishment, just blessing, especially if they are rebelling. If a teen rebels and you continue to punish, then all you do is make the child hate you every time you punish him. At that age you should be able to depend on your earlier training and discipline. If you're still giving a teenager a long list of do's and don'ts, you are making a mistake. When you cut down the number of rules, there is not as much to rebel against, and you allow them to move toward adulthood.

This doesn't mean you have no rules. You ought to have some house rules, and the children ought to respect them. But you should have fewer and fewer rules as they get older. For example, there ought to be fewer rules for a six-year-old than for a three-year-old; fewer rules for a nine-year-old than for a six-year-old; fewer rules for a twelve-year-old than a nine-year-old. As children get older, emphasize just three or four major areas, and break away from all the little things. In addition, each child needs to be treated individually.

It's important to discipline individually too. Don't apply the same discipline to every child. We had to spank our older son severely just to get his attention. Our younger son was much more sensitive—it took much less to get his attention.

In the seventies, long hair and sloppy clothes were in style. And my son's room was like a pigpen. But we chose not to fight over those things. So my son had long hair, and I'm sure he wore the same shirt for a solid week. He was probably one of the sloppiest people I ever knew during the high school years because that just wasn't one of the rules. We didn't make an issue of it, so it didn't become a problem.

He lived that way for two or three years. Then, when he got to college, he looked so bad that everybody started making fun of him. He had to shape up to fit in, so he started dressing better. When he got into real estate, his boss offered these observations: "Your hair looks awful; your suits look terrible; and your shoes are horrendous." The next day, he changed all of that. Now he is probably the best-dressed real estate broker in Dallas. His office is immaculate; his car is spotless; his yard is manicured. He wears white shirts, dark suits, and conservative ties daily. He thinks I'm a very liberal dresser.

SPIRITUAL LEADERSHIP

Both father and mother are responsible for the discipline of the children. But a father must take responsibility for the spiritual leadership in the home. If he doesn't, the children tend not to be very respectful toward God. This puts heavy responsibility on Christian fathers.

A father's influence is important because it helps a child to love God, the heavenly Father, if he respects his earthly father. Seldom do I find someone in prison who loves his father. Many hate their fathers. Because of this hatred, they do not respect authority.

> *A father must take responsibility for the spiritual leadership in the home.*

In Genesis 27:26, we read that Isaac said to his son Jacob, "Come near now and kiss me, my son." He wasn't talking to a child—Jacob was forty-five years old. Isaac's blessing involved a hug and a kiss and a word. He hugged and kissed his grown son, formalizing a lifetime habit. It seems to me that a father who draws his children close to him physically is much more likely to have the child stay close to him and follow his way of life.

A hug, a kiss, and a blessing is the Jewish concept in the Old Testament, and it has carried over into modern Judaism. Recently I visited a prison in Florida, and I asked one of the prison officials there how many Jews were in prison in Florida. He said thirteen. Only thirteen Jews in all the prisons in Florida! Florida has a high Jewish population, and there are forty thousand inmates in Florida prisons.

I began to ask the same question all over the country. I've discovered that in relation to the overall Jewish population, there is an infinitesimal number of them in jail or prison. One reason for this is that some of the hugging, kissing, touching, and blessing mentioned in the Old Testament has carried over to the modern-day Jew. They have a very strong sense of family. We, in the Judeo-Christian tradition, should have received this heritage. But I think we have been influenced more by the Prussian-German life-style, and also a sort of Puritanism that says don't touch anyone or show emotions.

My daughter is twenty-five years old. I find it very easy to hug and kiss her and bless her. It's a little tougher to hug and kiss my sons—who are not much older but are over six feet tall and 270 pounds! But I do it, and I think they need it and like it. I kiss them on the cheek and hug them, and I tell them I think they're fantastic. I think my blessing has created great inner strength in them they couldn't have had without it.

According to most authorities, 80 percent of troubled children do not get the blessing of their parents. As I've already mentioned, this can push them toward criminal activity. It also can predispose them toward becoming overachievers.

OVERACHIEVERS

The overachiever and the criminal probably spring from the same source. The one may become a great scientist or a great doctor while the other becomes a criminal. No one knows why. Even though he has achieved great success, the overachiever never quite feels accepted or acceptable.

One of the best examples of this is Kirk Douglas, who recently wrote a book called *The Ragman's Son*. In an interview on national television he was asked, "You've had such outstanding success; is there anything that you regret?"

Douglas answered, "Only one thing. I've never really gotten the blessing of the Ragman." That's the reason for the title of the book. Kirk Douglas's father never did anything more than sell rags on the streets of Philadelphia, yet Kirk Douglas and all of his children have become successful. But even after their outstanding success, he never gave them a blessing. And so there sat Kirk Douglas in his mid-seventies, with tears rolling down his cheeks saying, "If only the Ragman had blessed me." You may rationalize it; you may bury it; but you can never really outgrow the need for a parent's blessing.

MISSING THE BLESSING

If you've never received the blessing, you should forgive your parents. I met an inmate at a prison who told me, "I dig my dad up every morning before breakfast and beat him to death again, because I'm so angry with him that he never blessed me. He's been dead twenty years."

I said, "Well you've got to go to his grave in your imagination and forgive him, because he was dead wrong. He needs your forgiveness. Now you must go on with your life, and you have got to find someone who will bless you."

If your parents are alive, you should go to them and ask them for a blessing. If they refuse to give it to you, then you have to demand it. If they still refuse to give it to you, then you should seek it from someone else, perhaps your spouse, your minister, your friend, or someone you look up to and respect. This person should be someone whose blessing you feel is worthwhile. It may be a substitute father or mother, grandfather or grandmother.

> *Of course you can always seek the ultimate blessing, which is the blessing of God the heavenly Father through Jesus Christ the Son. That's the blessing everyone needs, but we also need an earthly blessing from a human being.*

Once, after a banquet, I was having a picture taken with a man. There wasn't anyone very close by, and so he whispered under his breath, "You know I'm sixty-three. My son is thirty-three, and I've never told him I love him."

I said, "Why don't you do it?"

"I will."

"When?"

"Tomorrow."

I said, "Do it tonight." And he agreed to try.

I was back in that city about three months later talking to a pastor of a church. He said, "One of the most outstanding young men in this church is that guy right back there on the third row. He is thirty-three years old. As far as I know, up until three months ago, he had never been in church in his life. But he came in on a Sunday night three months ago and almost immediately committed his life to the Lord. Now he's an outstanding Christian, and he's been one of the best things that has happened to this church in a long time." Then the pastor told me the young man's name—it was the son of the man I had stood next to at the banquet three months earlier.

I walked up to the young man and asked him about it. Here's what he told me. "My father came home and for the first time gave me his blessing. Right then I had an uncontrollable urge to get right with my heavenly Father, because for the first time I was right with my earthly father."

I think that is pretty typical—you don't get right with your heavenly Father until you are right with your earthly father. John the Baptist prepared the way of the Lord by turning the hearts of the fathers to their children (Luke 1:17). A new Christian father going home and blessing his children and blessing his wife can be the instrument by which they come to Jesus Christ.

THE DIFFERENCE BETWEEN "BLESSING" AND "AFFIRMATION"

Affirmation is a secular term that doesn't carry nearly the weight of the Jewish blessing.

The biblical blessing involved a touch, a warm word, and had an unconditional and permanent quality about it. It's not, "I'll bless you if you act right." It's, "I'll bless you unconditionally and forever, and there's nothing you can do about it. I'm not going to kick you out." The prodigal son came home after having been in a far country for many years, and the father gave him a ring and a robe and a blessing, unconditionally accepting him back.

That's what it's all about, men . . . being a blessing and giving the blessing at home. May God give you courage and strength to do what you know you should with your family.

■ GROWTH STRATEGIES ■

1. What do these verses teach about families and children?

   Psalm 127

   Psalm 128

   Proverbs 15:1

   Proverbs 19:18

   Proverbs 22:6

   Ephesians 4:1-7

Ephesians 6:4

Colossians 3:21

2. How would you describe the "blessing" to someone who knows very little about the Old Testament?

3. Why do you think some men have trouble expressing love (giving the blessing) to their children?

4. How did your father express his love and pass the blessing on to you?

5. What difference should being a Christian make in the way a father treats his children?

6. How can you improve the quality of time you spend with your children?

7. What steps can you take to convey your blessing on your children?

CHAPTER 11

WORK

Larry Kreider
President,
The Gathering / USA, Inc.

■ CHAPTER OBJECTIVE ■

To develop a godly view of work.

Several years ago I was driving my car at a snail's pace along a crowded freeway, only half listening to the music on the car radio. I was jolted into conscious thought by a song that didn't make sense. The tune was very familiar—"Whistle While You Work," sung by the famous seven dwarfs of Snow White fame. Only this time the lyrics were in Japanese.

The voice of the announcer came over the tune and said, "The Americans work to live; the Japanese live to work." I don't remember much about the commercial after that, because I was trying to figure out whether that was a true statement; and if it was true, who had the right philosophy, the Americans or the Japanese? This thought continued to worm its way through my mind until I had the opportunity to do serious investigative study on the subject of work. Here's some of what I learned.

DAILY WORK IS GOD'S IDEA

God is a worker. He loves work. In Genesis 1 we see God creating the heavens and the earth. The psalmist takes note of this creator God and declares, "I will praise the Lord with my whole heart, in the assembly of the upright and the congregation. The works of the Lord are great, studied by all who have pleasure in them. His work is honorable and glorious, and His righteousness endures forever" (Ps. 111:1-3).

After God created Adam and Eve, He placed them in the Garden of Eden, not to lounge eternally in perpetual paradise, but to work it and take care of it. This kind of work is obviously good and has nothing to do with sin. Eventually, sin will make work back-breaking, painful, unproductive, and unfulfilling at times, but work itself was not a product of sin.

The apostle Paul knew what it meant to work, and he expected other good Christians to do the same. He set himself up as a model, "For you remember, brethren, our labor and toil; for laboring night and day, that we might not be a burden to any of you, we preached to you the gospel of John" (1 Thess. 2:9–10). Then he told the Thessalonians, "to lead a quiet life, to mind your own business, and to work with your own hands, as we commanded you" (1 Thess. 4:11). If we read between the lines, we probably can hear Paul saying that no one is going to listen to anyone tell what God means to them if they aren't respected; and you can't be respected if you don't work.

Just in case some may want to play word games with Paul about what should be considered legitimate work, he gets quite specific and says that it should be honest work that is done well and that will provide enough to help others who are in need (Eph. 4:28).

There is a reward to this daily work. It has very little to do with the size of the paycheck, although that is not discounted entirely. The reward is the God-given capacity to experience joy (Eccl. 5:18-19). Several years ago, I was asked to give a brief speech at a Houston civic club on the subject of being thankful. They were probably looking for the traditional Thanksgiving devotional of gratitude for health, jobs, family, and country. I wanted to move beyond the obvious, so I took my cue from the book of Ecclesiastes. My conclusion was that the most blessed of the earth were those able to experience three conditions, all of which begin with a "C."

> *Solomon said that the capacity to enjoy a good meal, to be satisfied with his position in life, to have good health, and to receive more than ample wages was the greatest reward a man could hope for.*

The Capacity to Enjoy

This is the capacity to work, make a living, and enjoy the privileges that such work provides as a God-given gift. It is the ability to soak in the beauty of surrounding nature, to let our spirits soar with the sounds of majestic music, to be able to laugh and romp with a child—simple treasures often discarded as time-consuming annoyances in our clock-watching world. Solomon said that the capacity to enjoy a good meal, to be satisfied with his position in life, to have good health, and to receive more than ample wages was the greatest reward a man could hope for.

The Capability to Understand

This is the ability to make some sense out of life; to know what beliefs and values are worth holding on to; to understand who created the world, why it's so screwed up, and why there's no such thing as ultimate or pure happiness this side of heaven. It's the ability to realize that true spirituality is not the absence of conflict and to discern what issues are worthy of conflict. These are all gifts for those who have work and other priorities in their proper perspective.

The Compassion to Care

Compassion and caring are not created out of personal panic and chaos. The most compassionate people I know are also people of strength. They are people who work hard, who are productive, and who have deliberately decided the best way to distribute their resources to those who have needs.

ATTITUDES TOWARD EMPLOYMENT

Howard Dayton is a man I deeply admire. He is a very successful businessman who has committed all of his God-given talents and earthly resources to the Lord. Several years ago Howard started Crown Ministries, a small-group, financial-study organization. This was born out

of a burden to see men grasp the biblical mandates for handling their finances, to pursue the
goal of getting completely out of debt, and to
freely experience the joy of productive labor
that comes from a sense of God's calling.

Here's what he says on the subject of work, in
the introductory notes in his workbook.

> Over a fifty-year span, the average person
> spends 100,000 hours working. Most of an
> adult's life is involved in work, but often
> with the job comes some degree of dissatis-
> faction. Perhaps no statistic demonstrates
> the discontentment of Americans more than
> their job-hopping tendencies. A recent sur-
> vey found that the average man changes
> jobs every four and one-half years, the aver-
> age woman every three years.

All psychologists will tell you that attitudes
precipitate actions. A person can be dissatis-
fied with his or her work for many reasons.
Often it is a result of not knowing what the
Scriptures teach on the subject; not knowing
his particular skills or gifts; not taking the
time to figure out who is controlling his
attitude; or failing to establish attainable goals
for his life. Ultimately, we all have to take responsibility for our attitudes. If we are unhappy, we choose to be unhappy—or at least to
remain unhappy once we identify the root
cause.

God says the starting point in having a right
attitude is in realizing for whom you are really
working. Colossians 3:23-24 says, "And whatever you do, do it heartily, as to the Lord and
not to men, knowing that from the Lord you

will receive the reward of the inheritance; for you serve the Lord Christ." You may receive your paycheck from your boss, but the Lord hands out the report card. This perspective is found in several passages dealing with having a positive attitude toward labor.

> *God says the starting point in having a right attitude is in realizing for whom you are really working.*

A Christian should be highly motivated and industrious. The Bible says he should take his cue from the ants (Prov. 6:6-8). Ants don't require a supervisor to force them to work, their activity results in provisions for now and in the future. (If they are Japanese ants, they save 17 percent of their income; if they are American ants, they save 4 percent.)

A negative attitude toward work is implicitly condemned: "Whatever your hand finds to do, do it with your might; for there is no work or device or knowledge or wisdom in the grave where you are going" (Eccl. 9:10). (Don't be halfhearted.)

"Diligence is man's precious possession" (Prov. 12:27). (Don't be a quitter.)

"He who is slothful in his work is a brother to him who is a great destroyer" (Prov. 18:9).

The apostle Paul didn't cut any slack with those who were lazy. He told the Thessalonians, "If anyone will not work, neither shall he eat" (2 Thess. 3:10). So much for sugar-coated spiritual clichés! Paul's liberality didn't cover the slothful.

HISTORICAL PERSPECTIVE

The concept of work has gone through various stages since the beginning of the Church. Whatever your attitude toward work today, you can look back in history and find its source and those who also held that view.

For instance, the early Church was greatly influenced by the thoughts of the Greeks and Romans. Work was, at best, a necessary evil and was only good when it was freely chosen. Otherwise, a person was a slave and lacked personal autonomy. These views spilled over into the teachings of the Church where Augustine felt that the contemplative life had a higher value than the active life. This resulted in the idea that the highest calling of God was to move into a monastery with ample time for contemplation.

Along came the Reformers and the Puritans who rejected this "withdrawal from the world" approach. They developed four basic attitudes toward work that became the foundation for thought among nations that were distinctly influenced by the Christian viewpoint.

Attitude 1: The Sanctity of All Honorable Work

Those who held this view rejected a division between secular and sacred work. Martin Luther said clergymen were not engaged in more holy work than housewives and shopkeepers. "Household tasks have no appearances of sanctity: and yet these very works in connection with the household are more desirable than all the works of monks and nuns."

William Tyndale, who was burned at the stake for making English translations of the Bible, said, "There is no work better than another to please God; to pour water, to wash dishes, to be a cobbler, or an apostle, all is one."

These individuals believed that work—all work—was to be performed as an act of worship. No one said it more clearly than John Calvin: "Paul teaches that there is no part of our life or conduct, however insignificant, which should not relate to the glory of God."

Attitude 2: God Calls Every Person to His or Her Vocation

There are some who believe that only those who are called into full-time Christian work are strategically placed by God. Stanley Tamm in his book, *God Owns My Business* disagrees: "Although I believe in the application of good principles in business, I place far more confidence in the conviction that His purpose for me is in the business world. My business is my pulpit."

The practical result of this view is that it leads to contentment in our work. If a person really feels called to be a businessman, he no longer needs to feel like a second-class citizen in the kingdom. The Bible contains several views regarding calling.

View 1: *God calls certain persons to religious vocations, others are free to select any work.* An example of this is in Acts 13:2 where Paul and Barnabas were set aside by the Lord for special service.

View 2: *God calls all men to be Christians, but places of service depend on personal gifts and talents* (1 Cor. 12).

View 3: *God calls all men to be Christians, gives gifts to many for special Christian work, and calls a few to specific tasks.* In the Old Testament, you have the example of God calling Abraham to leave the Ur of the Chaldeans, or Moses to lead the children of Israel out of Egypt. In the New Testament, you have many examples of Christians being encouraged to use their talents and gifts as God gives opportunities (Rom. 12:6-8; 1 Cor. 12:4-10; Eph. 4:11; 1 Peter 4:10-11).

Attitude 3: The Motivation and Goals of Work

If you were to ask the average businessman in America what the primary goal of work is, he would probably answer, "to make money." This thought was set in concrete when Ben Franklin said, "Time is money," and "Early to bed, early to rise, makes a man healthy, wealthy, and wise." Although Ben may not have realized it, his thoughts downgraded the sanctity of the job itself, as well as volunteer work. This view seems to indicate that Bible study, family time, recreation, vacations, and other activities not affecting the bottom line of a financial statement are wasteful.

In the twentieth century, the technicalized world (which excludes very few nations) has carried Ben's thoughts even further. It concludes that economic survival is dependent not on just the simple premise that time has to be well invested in productive work, but also that survival will only be assured as nations move from the goal of economic necessity to economic freedom. In order to obtain this goal we have to become relentlessly future-oriented. No company survives without an aggressive Research and Development Department. This is all rightly justified in order to remain competitive in the marketplace. But there is a price to be paid—we are robbed of the daily joy of our labors.

As the Puritans looked at a pure motive for work, they concluded that it should meet six standards.

1. It should be useful for society.

2. It should glorify God.

3. It should be moral.

4. It should provide for the needs of the family.

5. It should use God-given talents.

6. It should provide a means to help the poor.

Attitude 4: A Sense of Moderation in Work

Laziness is not the real problem in our society; it carries a stiffer social stigma than drunkenness, sexual immorality, and other taboos of past generations. However, workaholism is the addiction that is running at epidemic proportions. The biblical view is found somewhere in between these two extremes. Martin Luther said, "God does not want me to sit at home, to loaf, to commit matters to God, and to wait till a fried chicken flies into my mouth. That would be tempting God."

So, we work and we work hard, but we keep things in perspective. We also know that Jesus said, "But seek first the kingdom of God and his righteousness, and all of these things shall be added to you" (Matt. 6:33).

The biblical approach is not to neglect the other priorities of life — our families, health, church, personal growth, and education. The Bible knows our frame, and it knows that if we have an inordinate lust for anything, then it will defile our spirit. The Lord gives a warning that should be heeded by all who bend toward a preoccupation with work: "It is vain for you to rise up early, to sit up late, to eat the bread of sorrows; for so He gives His beloved sleep" (Ps. 127:2).

A BIBLICAL PERSPECTIVE

This perspective has to do with a mandate that was given to Adam and Eve while they were in the garden—they were to subdue the earth (Gen. 1:28). This would involve a never-ending, lifelong process of tilling the soil, herding live-stock, building cities, working with metal and other mediums, and creating art and music. All of these vocations are mentioned in Genesis.

> *Man is created in God's image; and because*
> *God is seen as one who makes, forms,*
> *builds, and plants, He has touched all*
> *of labor with dignity.*

In spite of the fact that man sinned, he was to carry on this mandate even though there would be imperfect productivity, disappointment, and pain.

Man is created in God's image; and because God is seen as one who makes, forms, builds, and plants, He has touched all of labor with dignity. Nowhere is this more plainly seen than when God selected a man named Bezalel, of the tribe of Judah, to carry out the construction of the tabernacle in Exodus, chapters 35-36. "And He has filled him with the Spirit of God, in wisdom and understanding, in knowledge and all manner of workmanship, to design artistic works, to work in gold and silver and bronze, in cutting jewels for setting, in carving wood, and to work in all manner of artistic workmanship" (Ex. 35:31-33).

A FINAL PERSPECTIVE

When Jesus was on earth, it wasn't an accident that He came as a blue-collar worker, nor that His parables would deal with things like sowing seed, vineyard laborers, harvesters, house building, and swine tending. In Him there is no hierarchy of importance vocationally, there's only the wise use of the talents He dispenses. And according to the investment of these talents will we be rewarded or judged.

■ GROWTH STRATEGIES ■

1. What do these passages teach about the value of work?

    Genesis 1:28

    Genesis 2:1-3

    Exodus 35:30-33

    2 Thessalonians 3:10

2. What do these passages teach about how we should do our work?

    Proverbs 6:6-9

    Ecclesiastes 9:10

Ephesians 4:28

Colossians 3:23

3. Why should people work?

4. Why do you have the job you do? In other
    words, what criteria did you use in
    selecting that line of work?

5. In what areas of your work is it most
    difficult to live for Christ?

6.   If you were to "work for God and not for men" (Col. 3:23), what changes would you make on your job?

Personal and Progressive Commitment in Your Relationship to the Body of Christ

CHAPTER 12

IN THE FAMILY OF GOD: SMALL GROUPS

Jim Bankhead
Pastor, First Presbyterian Church,
Opelika, Alabama

■ CHAPTER OBJECTIVE ■

To show that sharing your faith and doubts, your joys and sorrows, your failures and progress with a few brothers and sisters in Christ is absolutely essential to healthy development as a believer. In fact, the Scriptures cannot be applied apart from close, vulnerable partnership relationships with others.

Wow! What strong conclusions. Let me share my reasons for them, and then you can decide these matters for yourself.

MY SPIRITUAL JOURNEY

I committed my life to Jesus Christ in junior high school. I was with my closest friends at a large meeting in Charlotte, North Carolina. At the end, the speaker gave an "invitation" to come forward.

The sharpest guy I knew was sitting next to me. Every girl I ever had a crush on, from grammar school to that point, somehow always wound up having a crush on him. I secretly felt that if I could be like him, then maybe, just maybe, a girl I liked would someday like me too.

During the invitation, I sensed from the top of my head to the bottom of my feet that I had to respond. It was deeper than an emotional experience. I immediately turned to my friend and said, "Let's go forward!"

He responded, "No! If you do that, you have to be a preacher or missionary!"

His reply threw me into an agonizing conflict. The possibility of being a missionary or preacher was like death to me. Committing my life to Christ seemed like a triple kind of death to me. I knew that if I got up, it was certain and immediate rejection by the friends I valued most and from whom I most wanted acceptance. It also meant an uncertain and painful future. Of course, I did not understand all of this back then. But I did feel the pain as fully as anyone could feel it. It was a real life-and-death struggle. I had tried to avoid rejection; I could not avoid a decision. So this was the deepest dilemma of my youth. For several minutes I sat paralyzed.

Finally, with tears streaming down my cheeks, I stood up, pushed by my friend and all the others on that row, and went forward. Even now I vividly remember the warmth of acceptance by God that I sensed deep inside. But I also remember the deep feelings of rejection and loneliness as later I waited in the parking lot for my friends. I ached inside, feeling totally isolated and cut off from them. Those feelings were so deep that years later when I would hear evangelistic messages and invitations, I would become nauseated. None of us talked about these feelings and thoughts back then. I didn't know until just a few years ago that two other friends had followed me forward.

Back home I didn't know what to do. My mother was a devout Christian, but I didn't even know how to talk with her about my commitment to Christ. I felt totally alone. The preacher and members of my church never talked about their faith in any personal way outside church. So I told no one.

No one in my hometown seemed to involve themselves with others very deeply. This was especially true for me. I can remember no one talking about personal needs and issues of faith.

I do remember completing the follow-up literature from the crusade organization. I loved being guided in reading and studying the Bible, and I had a lot of questions. But no one seemed available to help me find solid answers. I prayed in secret the best I could. And I began trying to live the way the Bible directed.

I knew I did not want to just play at being a Christian. I wanted to learn to be the real thing, whatever that was. But I felt all alone in my efforts to live out my commitment to Christ. I was a very private person, especially with the deeper things that were going on inside me.

In my secret journey of faith, I progressed fairly well through high school. But college was a different story. There, everything about my faith was tested. I didn't know what was hitting me, but I was totally unprepared for these "tests of faith." I flunked them all miserably.

By my junior year, I had all but concluded that God must not be real. I was afraid to adopt that position fully, but secretly this was how I felt. Of course I was quite confused about where Jesus fit in. So again I found myself in a dilemma.

I could not shake loose from the bond of faith that had been formed years before, but I was confused and totally out of sync with that bond. I wanted to believe, but I didn't have a clue as to what to do with my unbelief.

THE RECOVERY

The recovery began near the end of my junior year as I sensed that either I had to get my heart released from its bond of faith or get my head straight and in line with my heart. I had no idea how it would happen. I just knew I was going to have to go one way or the other. Being stuck in the middle, unable to move forward or backward, was miserable.

I had never veered off the path of faith, but I was only semi-conscious of God's presence. I had quit reading my Bible because of so many unanswered questions, and I had all but stopped going to church. Prayer was an empty and meaningless exercise. On the outside, everything probably looked fine, but on the inside, something was terribly wrong. I had no idea how to correct what was out of line, but I knew that something was not right.

Many factors worked together in the restoration and recovery of my relationship with God. First of all, I met men who openly shared their faith and also their struggles with God. I had never been around men who did that. I only knew women who shared that deeply and honestly.

In addition, I was able to scrutinize the lives of some new friends who professed faith in Jesus Christ. Also, I began to want to find out what had gone wrong for me, so I started identifying the questions that had piled up within me. And I re-established contact with a local church.

The two most critical factors in my recovery developed when I fell in love with the girl who eventually became my wife. The deep rejection and trauma I experienced with her tapped into my buried feelings of rejection about my faith. For the first time, I had to face the fact that I didn't have what it took to work through our relational problems. In this critical crisis of the heart, my inner being was cracked open to the core. Not knowing what to do, I became desperate. Faith was no longer merely an intellectual exercise, because I needed help to survive. Having exhausted my resources, I began to cry out: "God! If you are real, please help me!" Slowly, but surely, help appeared.

This stress and helplessness pushed me back to the Bible, but in a new way. Slowly, God's Word began to come alive to me. No longer was it a book about a particular religion. Instead it was a survival manual to guide me through this turbulent relational storm. I was helped to develop skills in reading and studying it for myself. No longer dependent upon someone else to tell me what it said or meant, I began to examine and test it for myself.

As my heart was cracked open, a second critical event occurred, I developed a new kind of friendship with an older Christian. This friend helped me pour out my heart and all its secrets . . . my hurt, confusion, doubts, and anger. I hadn't realized what was buried deep inside. She showed me mercy, tenderness, acceptance, encouragement, and wisdom. For the first time I had someone who could help me share my heart.

Frankly, I was shocked to discover how much had built up over the years. Through this friend, God began to work deep healing in my relationship with the woman I loved. Central to my recovery of faith in Jesus Christ was having my heart forced open and having a caring, accepting, understanding, and forgiving friend who heard its contents. She showed me the love of Christ in the clearest and most practical ways possible.

Other things began to accelerate my recovery. As I faced my buried questions and hidden feelings, I began to grow in my confidence to find believable answers. Thomas became my favorite disciple, because I knew I also would not be able to believe if I did not "see with my own eyes" the verifying evidence for the claims of Scripture.

Another buried disappointment centered upon the church. It had been a pretty dull experience for me growing up. And church workers appeared to have no fun or enjoyment in life. But now I was around Christian workers who enjoyed life fully. They helped me have fun, perhaps for the first time. I didn't know you could have so much fun in a Christian setting.

I was like a semi-conscious man with smelling salts thrust under his nose. Slowly but surely my own faith began to revive. I was now conscious in my faith, but only sitting up in the middle of the path. Others were walking around me, alive, healthy, attractive, and enjoying life. They were making great progress in following Christ. I was not yet sure exactly how to get up, but I knew that I had to do whatever it took. I had a real hope that I could recover.

Then I was given the privilege of being a part of a church that had a vitality among its members and officers that I had not seen before. I began to read the writings of those who had wrestled through many of the same questions I had. The primary feeling that began to build up within me was, "I am not alone nor the only one who has had problems in believing." For the first time, I understood that the sense of being alone and isolated was at the heart of why I stumbled. Now my recovery was full. I was accepted and encouraged as a "believer" by a host of others. Standing up in my faith, I was excited and alive again, and I was eager to move forward.

I recovered, because I was no longer alone. I realized that I had brothers and sisters with whom I could discuss my issues of faith and also share my doubts and not be rejected. All my problems were not solved, but for the first time I knew, felt, and experienced that I wasn't alone. I felt a real part of a caring, supportive, and assisting "family in Christ."

TWENTY YEARS LATER

Twenty years have passed during which I have carefully studied and researched why people make genuine commitments of their lives to Jesus Christ, but then stumble and make such little progress afterwards. One of the main reasons is that they become isolated from a meaningful "family connection" with other growing believers. To grow in the faith, we need the personal and practical care of other maturing believers.

Never forget that your initial commitment to Christ was just the beginning. A newborn Christian needs the personal care and attention of older believers who know the "ins" and "outs" of how to grow in Christ . . . a "family of faith."

> *Never forget that your initial commitment to Christ was just the beginning.*

Although there are times when God calls you to go alone, He never intends for you to travel that way very long. God's help most often comes through the personal and practical assistance of others, especially older brothers and sisters in the faith, and not just from the preacher and pastoral staff.

THE FIRST SMALL GROUP

Jesus formed the "Church" in the Gospels. He gave it shape and character. He fashioned it to be His "family of disciples." In the New Testament, a family of faith was like a biological family, usually beginning as a small group. This "spiritual family" was the structure Jesus formed to support and guide the healthy development of His young disciples. Jesus trained, equipped, and empowered older believers as "disciple-leaders." He charged them to tend to and guide younger followers.

To appreciate what the New Testament says God intends the Church to be, we must understand what the Church is not. It is not a building made of bricks and mortar. It is not a once-a-week meeting for public worship or Sunday school. It is not a religious institution that offers religious programs to its members and the public. These are the cultural forms of the Church today in many countries.

> *For healthy disciple-growth to continue today, it is critical for you to be a part of this same kind of small, "brother and sister" group.*

In the New Testament, a local church started as something quite different from these cultural forms. It began as a small group of brothers and sisters who supported and assisted each other in following Jesus Christ.

For healthy disciple-growth to continue today, it is critical for you to be a part of this same kind of small, "brother and sister" group. As you recover this New Testament pattern for being and building the Church, you too will mature and grow in your knowledge of and faith in Jesus Christ.

THEIR "DEVOTIONS"

One of the main passages that explains the pattern of how Jesus set up the church to function is Acts 2:41-47. It says of the new disciples in Jerusalem:

> *Then those who gladly received his word were baptized; and that day about three thousand souls were added to them. And they continued steadfastly in the apostles' doctrine and fellowship, in the breaking of bread, and in prayers. Then fear came upon every soul, and many wonders and signs were done through the apostles. Now all who believed were together, and had all things in common, and sold their possessions and goods, and divided them among all, as anyone had need. So continuing daily with one accord in the temple, in breaking bread from house to house, they ate their food with gladness and simplicity of heart, praising God and having favor with all people. And the Lord added to the church daily those who were being saved.*

Acts 2:42 lists the things to which the members of the first small groups of disciples were devoted.

1.   The apostles' teaching

     In Matthew 28:20, when Jesus charged these apostles to make disciples of all people, He included the responsibility of "teaching them to observe all things that I have commanded you." The members of these first small groups devoted themselves to learning how to obey Jesus' commands.

2. *Koinonia*, or the fellowship

    This word also referred to business partnerships. At times it is used for intimate, caring relationships. The members of these first small groups apparently worked at intimate sharing and partnership in following Christ together. They were not alone. They were partners in discipleship.

3. The breaking of bread

    They shared their meals together, enjoying social fellowship. This was a common practice among Jews of the first century. The first small groups met to eat together and to enjoy social fellowship around meals.

4. Prayer

    The members of these first disciple-groups prayed individually and together in their groups. They opened their hearts to their Lord when they met together.

These four "devotions" are what you should be working on by yourself and with others, one-on-one and in small groups.

MY EFFORTS TO APPLY THESE DEVOTIONS

I saw that in the New Testament the first disciples met together in small groups to work on these four disciple-devotions, but I didn't know how. I also was unsure how to join with others.

I prayed for God to introduce me to at least one Christian friend with whom I could work on doing these four things. The day I prayed for this, a young elder in our church invited me to have a cup of coffee after a Wednesday night program. Initially I turned him down, forgetting all about my prayer. As he walked out of my office, I suddenly remembered what I had prayed and wondered if he might be the friend I needed.

I jumped up and ran out into the hall. He was almost out the door of the church when I caught him. I said I changed my mind and asked if he was still interested in coffee. He said, "Sure!" This started a friendship that changed my life and walk in Christ profoundly.

I was not exactly sure what to do, but I knew what the first disciples did, and so I secretly committed myself to doing the same with this new friend. At first, I didn't tell him why I was doing this. Frankly, I was afraid he might reject me if I did.

We began to share our struggles in living out the Christian faith. He kept asking, "How do I apply what I'm hearing on Sundays to the rest of the days of the week?" I wasn't sure, but I joined him in working to discover the answer. Since then, this question has been the heart of my journey as a Christian.

Later, he invited me to be a part of a small, Tuesday breakfast group that had been meeting for over a year. They ate, studied, discussed, and prayed together. I had met with this same group the year before but had lost interest after a short time and had dropped out. I had not seen the significance or importance of such a support group.

But then I realized that this was an opportunity to follow the New Testament pattern. Therefore, I entered into this second opportunity with a renewed commitment to learn and contribute as much as I could to our shared discipleship. This small group, along with my one-on-one relationship with one of its members, set my life on an irreversible course of following Christ with others.

I soon discovered the truth of Ecclesiastes 4:9-12: "Two are better than one, because they have a good reward for their labor. For if they fall, one will lift up his companion. But woe to him who is alone when he falls, for he has no one to help him up. Again, if two lie down together, they will keep warm; but how can one be warm alone? Though one may be overpowered by another, two can withstand him. And a threefold cord is not quickly broken."

I began to see that Jesus usually sent out those first disciples in pairs. In Acts, this "pairing" strategy continues. Peter and John always appear together—they are hardly ever alone. Barnabas and Paul traveled and ministered together. They recruited others to travel and minister with them. In many of the cities, they left behind small groups of disciples, and they appointed a smaller group of elders to oversee the development and growth of these younger disciples. Slowly but surely, I began to see small groups following the pattern of Acts 2:42 as Jesus' and the Holy Spirit's way of building the Church.

Then I began to see that churches in the New Testament always began as small groups of men and women who believed that Jesus is the Messiah and who joined together to grow in their knowledge, understanding, and obedience to Him. Paul's teaching on "the Body of Christ" began to make more sense as I realized he was referring to a "group of Jesus' disciples."

"For as the body is one and has many members, but all the members of that one body, being many, are one body, so also is Christ. For by one Spirit we were all baptized into one body — whether Jews or Greeks, whether slaves or free — and have all been made to drink into one Spirit. For in fact the body is not one member by many (1 Cor. 12:12–14).

"But, speaking the truth in love, many grow up in all things into Him who is the head — Christ — from whom the whole body, joined and knit together by what every joint supplies, according to the effective working by which every part does its share, causes growth of the body for the edifying of itself in love" (Eph. 4:15-16).

Paul's whole ministry centered upon forming these small disciple "bodies" or groups. It was these little "gatherings of disciples" that came to be called "churches." His goal for these groups was to present every member "perfect in Christ Jesus" (Col. 1:28).

I became convinced that being a part of a small family or group of disciples was essential in the maturing of the first disciples. Could it be any different today?

PERSONAL CONCLUSIONS

For anything to grow, there must be an environment or atmosphere that stimulates, feeds, and supports that growth. For human beings to grow and develop properly, there must also be older, more experienced people who support, encourage, and tend to that growth. For healthy maturing of the human personality there must be a healthy connection or bond with other people.

Without personal attention and a healthy connection, barriers and hindrances will stunt and retard healthy development. This is surely what happened to me in my Christian development. My growth was arrested because of no personal attention and no healthy connection to older, healthy believers.

People also do not grow properly without both an internal and external support structure. The human body has to have a skeleton.

This is the human body's internal support structure. The internal support structure for a Christian is God's Word: the commands, promises, and disciplines of Jesus.

To grow up properly, a person also has to have an external support structure. This is the family. Both the skeleton and the family, when healthy, provide strong yet flexible support internally and externally. To develop in a healthy manner, these same things have to be present for Christians. Disciples of Jesus Christ also need the internal support of God's Word and external support of a healthy "family of faith."

Also, to grow properly in Christ, you must learn to schedule your time the way Jesus did. You need time alone with the Lord and with other believers. This time with others must be personal and practical, and not just in a public, impersonal worship service. You will therefore need to spend time productively one-on-one, with a group of two, three, or four, and in a larger group of believers. This time with others is principally for your nurture and development. Times alone with the Lord along with one-on-one and small-group times are essential to spiritual growth.

Small groups come in many forms. Yours may be a Sunday school class, a share and prayer group, or a Bible study group. Whatever the size, you will need to see it as time for personal and practical attention to the things of Christ. It is the time to learn to carry out Jesus' commands with the support and assistance of other Christians. Some of this time should be spent practicing and working on the "devotions" of Acts 2:42.

Also, many of Jesus' commands are "one another" commands. They are to be applied in your relationships. Obviously, "one another" commands cannot be practiced alone; therefore, to grow stronger, you will need to practice them with others.

Remember, the New Testament church was a group of disciples. The church is properly called a fellowship of maturing disciples. It was not limited to worship services held on Sundays.

Today, small groups are the most efficient and effective structures for both learning and being trained to obey Jesus' commands personally and practically.

BUILDING PERSONAL RELATIONSHIPS WITH OTHERS

We know that babies do not grow and mature in isolation. They are born into families. The parents and older brothers and sisters oversee the development of the younger family members.

We also know that to grow and mature physically and psychologically, the family structure must be healthy. In a healthy family, parents and older brothers and sisters nurture, support, train, and discipline the younger family members so that they also can grow to maturity. Such personal attention in a family structure is essential to healthy growth. Neglect stunts and retards a child's development.

The same is true for development in obeying Jesus' commands.

> *A mark of Christian maturity is actively sharing and growing in extending the ministry of Christ to others in the world.*

Individual attention, encouragement, correction, and training occur best one-on-one and in a small fellowship. Such a fellowship needs to be led by at least one older, maturing disciple.

THE WORKING DYNAMICS

What makes a healthy one-on-one relationship? What are the dynamics that build a healthy small group? What dynamics need to be present to spur healthy growth and development in and among believers?

Jesus pressed specific dynamics into the lives and relationships of the first disciples. To function today, Christians must work to provide these same dynamics for one another. We must work together to build an atmosphere of:

- honesty and sincerity (Eph. 4:15)

- love and forgiveness (John 15:12)

- support and encouragement (1 Thess. 5:11)

- confession and correction (James 5:16)

- accountability and submission (Eph. 5:21)

- impartiality and welcome (James 2:6-9 and Rom. 15:7).

These are the working dynamics of the body of Christ. They are the basic ingredients which together form God's atmosphere of healing grace and truth.

Jesus lived these dynamics with the twelve disciples. He pressed these upon them when they didn't know how to live. After the Holy Spirit came upon them in Acts, they lived these same dynamics with the new disciples they made. They pressed them upon the larger group just as Jesus had done with them. In the New Testament, Jesus makes it clear that He intends these to be the working dynamics of His Church or body.

For these to become the qualities in your life, you have to make a clear decision to live them out in all your relationships, especially with all other group members. For even with the best of intentions, these dynamics do not automatically occur in a person's life, in a small group, or in a local church. Sometimes it takes years of obedience to Christ for these traits to become fully operational among fellow Christians.

Jesus started by working them into the small group of His disciples. As the group grew in size, the nucleus of four and the leader-core of twelve pressed these same dynamics into the larger congregation of disciples.

You will need to do this whether anyone else in your group or church does so or not. Someone has to set these dynamics as the primary pace for a smaller group and the rest of the church to follow and imitate. You have to make sure, as Jesus did, that these dynamics are pressed into your own personality first and then upon and into the character of the whole group. So you be the one to set the pace.

Then look for one or two friends with whom you can share your life and walk in Christ. Work to build the devotions and these dynamics of Christ into your relationships with them. As you do this, you will discover the truth of Jesus' promise in Matthew 18:20, "For where two or three are gathered together in My name, I am there in the midst of them."

■ GROWTH STRATEGIES ■

1. What do these passages teach about
    Christians encouraging and supporting
    each other?

    Ecclesiastes 4:9-12

    1 Corinthians 12:12-14

    Ephesians 4:15-16

    Colossians 1:28

    1 Thessalonians 5:11

2. What do these passages imply about small
    groups?

    Matthew 18:20

Acts 2:42

3. What structure or program does your church have that fosters accountability and support?

4. With whom do you have a deep, supportive relationship?

5. What might you do to become involved in a vital and close small group?

6. If no group currently exists, what could
    you do to find one or start one?

CHAPTER 13

THE CHURCH

Dr. Jay Kesler
President, Taylor University

■ CHAPTER OBJECTIVE ■

I won't pretend to be able to answer all your questions about churches in these few pages. Instead, my goal is to give you some basic direction and guidelines.

Drive through any town in America, and you'll see scores of churches, in every shape, size, just about every conceivable denomination. There are German Baptists, Swedish Lutherans, Korean Presbyterians, Roman Catholics, African Methodist Episcopalians, Greek Orthodox, and on and on the list goes. Choosing a specific church to attend can seem like an impossible task.

I will use a question-and-answer format. These are the questions most frequently asked about church. Maybe you've been asking them too. Read the chapter straight through, or find the questions most appropriate to your situation.

WHY DO WE HAVE CHURCHES?

From my reading of the Bible, I find that the church is the only institution that was actually instituted by Jesus Christ. In Matthew 16:15-18 you'll find that Jesus asked Peter to summarize His teachings and who He was. Peter answered, "You are the Christ, the Son of the living God." Then Jesus looked at Peter and said, "On this rock I will build My church, and the gates of Hades shall not prevail against it" (Matt. 16:15-18).

Throughout history, there has been a good deal of discussion about what Jesus meant by the "rock." Many Bible scholars believe Jesus was saying that upon that profession of faith or upon a man like Peter who professes the kind of faith he professed, Jesus would build His Church. That is, Jesus was saying, "I will put together a group of people in a configuration I will call a church, and hell will not be able to withstand it." So the Church of Jesus Christ was begun by Christ and is the one institution that He holds dearest to His heart.

Of course it's important to remember that there are two meanings for the word "church." One has to do with the gathered church or the local church, the group of believers in a particular community or neighborhood who gather together in the name of Jesus. This group has programs and meetings, and there are certain instructions in the New Testament about it. Christians, for example, are told not to forsake the gathering of themselves together (Heb. 10:25). And we know by example that the early church gathered together on the first day of the week (Acts 20:7; 1 Cor. 16:2). We also have rather specific biblical knowledge as to what they did—they sang hymns and songs, broke bread, and so forth (Acts 2:46-47; Col. 3:16). This constitutes the gathered church or the "local church."

> *The church of Jesus Christ was begun by Christ and is the one institution that He holds dearest to His heart.*

Then there's the "invisible" or "universal" Church. This refers to all the people on the face of the earth who claim Jesus Christ as Savior and Lord. They are brothers and sisters, according to biblical terminology, and they form an invisible, worldwide network. These are the citizens of Christ's Kingdom and, of course, there is great national, cultural, economic, racial, and political diversity. The Church is the way God chose to preserve His teachings in the world and perpetuate His message. It's not just a conservation task or "Hold the fort, for I am coming." Rather it is an aggressive movement, more like "Onward Christian Soldiers." Remember that Jesus told Peter that the gates of hell would not prevail against it. In other words, hell would not be able to stand against the power of the Church. The Church will attack evil. There will be open warfare with the prince of this world, the prince of darkness.

So when a person becomes a Christian, he really doesn't have an option whether or not he is going to be part of the Church of Jesus Christ. On one level, he is a part of the invisible Church, by definition, because he knows Christ as Savior. Then, if he is obedient to Christ, he will gather with other believers to carry on the important functions (preaching, teaching, partaking of the Lord's supper, fellowshipping, praying, etc.) until Christ returns.

WHY SHOULD I BE INVOLVED IN A LOCAL CHURCH?

There are people who say "Christ yes, Christianity no"; or "I want to have a private faith. I don't want to be part of a church." But we're instructed to be part of a church, and there's a tremendous amount of New Testament teaching on the subject. For instance, Paul compares the Church to a body (the "body of Christ") and talks about the importance of all the members (1 Cor. 12:12-31; Eph. 4:1-16). In fact, it could be said that when a person receives Christ as Savior, this is the last individual act he ever performs. From that moment on, through the work of the Holy Spirit, he is a part of the body of Christ. His strengths are added to the Church, and his weaknesses are compensated for by others in the Church.

In the New Testament, there is nothing taught about individual wholeness, in the modern sense of the term, that is, that man is autonomous and self-contained. We only have wholeness through Jesus Christ; and when we have wholeness in Christ, there is a body wholeness whereby the body is made complete by the complementary gifts that God has given each of His children.

And, of course, this larger body of believers, the Church, can be found gathered in small, local congregations . . . churches.

> *You need the Church, and the Church needs you.*

HOW CAN I CHOOSE A CHURCH?

In choosing a local church to join or become involved in, the first thing to look for is a church that finds its authority in the Scriptures. By that I mean they believe that the Bible is not symbolic or just informative, but is the authoritative Word of God in every area of life. It is trustworthy and is the guide for faith and behavior.

After this, there are other criteria that are much less important and yet may be important to individuals. Does the program appeal to one's own need to know and worship God? Does the service enhance one's sense of reverence and worship and one's desire to follow God? People raised with a certain musical taste will feel more comfortable in a church with that kind of music.

Other personal criteria involve programs that the churches offer. If a person has small children, going to a church that has a well-formed Christian Education program would be a good idea. There's ebb and flow in people's lives and there are different needs at different times in their lives. There's a certain kind of church that might be attractive to a couple while their children are very small, and perhaps another kind of church that would have more appeal when their children are teenagers. I'm not suggesting that a person change churches when his or her family's needs change (there's great value in being committed to a specific body of believers over the long haul), but these would be contributing factors.

Even proximity has some practical value. When a church is close, a person can get involved in the programs without having to drive a great distance.

You choose a church not only for yourself, but for your family and their needs.

WHAT IF CHURCH GETS BORING?

This question betrays a kind of basic misunderstanding of the nature of the local church. The purpose of church services is to worship God, remembering God's gift to us through Jesus Christ. So when someone says he doesn't get anything out of church or that it bores him, he betrays a lack of understanding of the purpose of the local church.

You see, God has done everything for us. He created us, revealed Himself to us through the Bible, sent Jesus to die on the cross in our place for our sins, and gave us the opportunity to have eternal life through Christ. A church service, specifically worship, should not be the place where we look for more from God. It should be a place where we give to Him . . . our adoration and appreciation for who He is and for what He has done. So it's not so much a matter of I don't get anything out of it, because I've already gotten everything out of it. God has done everything for me.

> *In other words, true worship is not man-centered, but God-centered. We should attend church to worship God, not to make ourselves feel happy or more entertained.*

Ultimately, even Christian education and preaching is really about learning more about God so we can worship Him with greater fidelity and bring more honor to His name.

Church is where we go to participate and to give back, rather than to get. Obviously, everyone would like to find a place where this can be done in a pleasant setting. But not finding the ideal church does not give us the right to say, "Well I just won't attend, because I don't get anything out of it."

WHAT ABOUT ALL THE HYPOCRITES IN CHURCH?

Someone has said rather wisely that you have to be smaller than a hypocrite to hide behind one. That sounds clever, but in a sense it is true.

Another way to say that is, you cannot have a counterfeit of anything without actually having the real thing. A counterfeit dollar has no meaning at all unless there is something that is called a real dollar bill. If there is not a real dollar somewhere, then what you call a counterfeit is not a counterfeit—it's a unique something in itself, but it doesn't counterfeit anything else. So, the fact that there are hypocrites in the church simply shows that there is "the real thing," that God is real and His standards are real. In other words, you cannot have outrage against imperfection unless there is some idea of perfection. There has to be an idea of perfection before there can be imperfection.

This is why the Scriptures carefully encourage us not to look to men as our heroes or ultimate examples. In fact, the presupposition of the Bible is that people are imperfect, finite and sinful, and so they will act imperfectly. Therefore, we should keep our eyes on Jesus, the Author and Finisher of our faith (Heb. 12:2), as opposed to watching fallible human beings.

Instead of worrying about the hypocrisy in others, we should deal with hypocrisy in our own lives and attempt to be conformed more and more into the image of God's Son (Rom. 8:29). Hypocrites have nothing to do with it.

BUT WHAT IF THE CHURCH NO LONGER MEETS MY NEEDS?

If this is your question, first you should examine your own life. Perhaps church doesn't meet your needs because you have lost sight of the reasons for going to church. Are you there to be entertained? Have you begun to compare the church to some idea based on entertainment, fun, and pleasure?

The only legitimate reason I think a person could use to say that a church doesn't meet his needs is that it has stopped communicating the Word of God and is no longer faithful to the Word of God. That is, the church is unfaithful to the content or to the spirit of Scripture and is going in a direction that is inconsistent with God's Word.

If that's the case, either he should try to change the church from the inside, or he should seek another church that is closer to the Word of God in content, lifestyle, and attitude.

HOW ABOUT THE REST OF THE FAMILY?

Only a very unusual church will meet all the needs of a broadly based family with small children, parents in mid-life, and adolescents. In this case, as with virtually everything else in life, there's a kind of a balancing act, a weighing of comparative values and decisions. My personal feeling is that because life is so volatile and so difficult for adolescents, if the church is meeting the needs of the adolescent who is more changeable and more insecure than the parent, the parent should sacrifice his well-being, at least temporarily, for the sake of the young person. But this is the choice each person and each family would have to make. I think in the long run, most families would be well served if they made the choice toward the young person rather than toward the adult.

WHAT SHOULD I DO IF MY WIFE WANTS TO GO TO ANOTHER CHURCH?

Just as in the situation above where we discussed choosing a church for the sake of an adolescent, there's an important biblical principle to consider here—the unity between the husband and wife. This unity should be considered above personal preference. In other words, sometimes the believer should make compromises in order to maintain or bring about unity in the family.

I could conceive of a situation where a wife is deeply ingrained in a church for a lifetime; and perhaps her family has been deeply involved in it, with deep ethnic and social ties. In that case, the husband should probably suppress his personal preference in order to maintain that important social connection. It would be better for the husband to stay in that church and meet his needs in an informal Bible study or in some other Bible class. There is room for compromise and flexibility.

When you accepted Christ as your personal Savior, you became "born again" and "adopted" into God's family, with many brothers and sisters. As such, you are an important member of the universal Church, the body of Christ. Your brothers and sisters need you and your special gifts, talents, and personality. And you need them.

The family meets regularly on Sunday for worship, instruction, encouragement, and fellowship. Choose a local church and get involved.

■ GROWTH STRATEGIES ■

1. What do these passages teach about the
    local church?

    Hebrews 10:25

    Acts 20:7

    Acts 2:46-47

    Colossians 3:16

    1 Corinthians 12:12-31

2. Describe the church service you remember
    enjoying the most.

3.   What keeps you from

      a. going to church?

      b. becoming more involved in church?

4.   What did you get out of church last
      Sunday?

5.   What did you give at church last Sunday?

6.   Assuming the time and opportunity, in
      what area of service could you make your
      best contribution to your local church?

Personal and Progressive Commitment to the Work of Christ in the World

CHAPTER 14

BEING HIS WITNESSES

Dr. Charles Colson
Author, speaker, former special counsel to President Nixon
Chairman of Prison Fellowship Ministries

■ CHAPTER OBJECTIVE ■

The goal of evangelism is to persuade men and women to become disciples of Jesus Christ and to serve Him in the fellowship of His church.
—Lausanne Committee on Evangelism

What went through Maximilian Kolbe's mind when he volunteered to lay down his life for prisoner #5659?

No one knows, but that decision was the natural consequence of a character shaped by a life-long commitment to Christ. *What he did resulted from who he was.*

The moral of Maximilian Kolbe's story applies to every believer: What we do results from who we are. Being precedes doing. Central to our Christian witness in the world lies the reality of who we are individually in relationship to God and to one another in the new society of God's people—the Church.

Jesus calls us to *be* a witness. Just before His ascension, He told His disciples: "But you shall receive power when the Holy Spirit has come upon you; and you shall be witnesss to me in

Jerusalem, and in all Judea and in Samaria, and to the end of the earth" (Acts 1:8).

Many Christians interprest these words as *to* witness, rather than to *be* a witness. They see it as an activity rather than the state of our very being. This is particularly so among evangelicals, for whom "witnessing" has become the supreme duty, and a source of enormous pressure.

Once a friend of mine, Charlie, and some others went to witness in a local bar, armed with "Four Spiritual Laws" pamphlets. Charlie struck up a conversation with a typical "yuppie" who soon admitted his spiritual emptiness. As Charlie told the man of his own experience with Christ, the rapport between them deepened. Sensing that the man was not ready for a commitment, Charlie took his phone number and made plans to contact him later.

After they left the bar, one of the others asked Charlie, "Did you go through the book with him?"

"No," Charlie replied. "He wasn't ready. We're going to talk again later."

The young man was furious and exploded, "Here we are trying to witness, and you didn't even go through the book!" Six months later this same young man had a nervous breakdown. We may have many opportunities *to* witness, but Jesus charges us to *be* witnesses.

> *We may have many opportunities to witness, but Jesus charges us to be witnesses.*

To understand that is wonderfully liberating! It is also intensely demanding. Remember Francis of Assisi's challenge: "Preach the Gospel all the time; if necessary, use words."

How are we Christ's witnesses? With our *whole* being. This includes responsiveness to the Holy Spirit, our best judgment, and sensitivity to other people. We often miss the balance and tilt to one extreme or the other.

Unfortunately, those who lack balance are the ones the world stereotypes as the church—the employee with a Jesus coffee mug and spouts Christian platitudes but does the shoddiest work in the office; the businessman who prays before every meeting and then cheats his customers; the pro-life activist who wears a "God Loves You" button while hurling invectives at women entering abortion clinics.

For the watching world, it is difficult to separate the message from these messengers. Or, as Sheldon Van Auken put it:

"The best argument for Christianity is Christians: their joy, their certainty, their completeness. But the best argument *against* Christianity is also Christians—when they are somber and joyless, when they are self-righteous and smug in complacent consecration, when they are narrow and repressive, then Christianity dies a thousand deaths."[1]

At the other extreme are those who earnestly live their faith but never articulate the reason for their hope. While people may look at us and see a reflection of Christ, and even admire the reflection, they may never know the source of our joy unless we tell them about Him.

We must always remember that our first calling is to *be* a witness, but that an element of that calling is our duty to *proclaim* a witness. Because the Gospel is propositional, proclaiming it is a primary task of the church.

TO PROCLAIM THE GOOD NEWS

Evangelism comes from the Greek verb *euangelizomai*, "to announce or proclaim or bear good news."

Every believer is called to bear the Good News of God's saving love for men and women, but not all are called to be evangelists. The latter is a specific office commissioned for the good of the church and filled by those gifted by God for that task. The book of Acts is full of the evangelistic fervor of the early church, including the adventures of the greatest evangelist—the apostle Paul.

One of the most remarkable evangelists in the history of the church was a man whose memory is associated more with shamrocks and leprechauns than the proclamation of the Gospel—Patrick of Ireland.

Kidnapped as a teenager, Patrick was taken from his wealthy home in Roman Britain in

405 A.D., transported to Ireland, and sold to a farmer as a shepherd.

Patrick had grown up in a strong Christian home, but the faith had not been real to him until one day, tending sheep in the barren hills of Ireland, he encountered the Great Shepherd and purposed to follow Him. Eventually Patrick escaped from slavery, returned to Britain, and became a priest. Then in a dream he heard an Irish voice pleading with him: "Holy boy, we are asking you to come home and walk among us again."

Return to the land of his servitude? Unlikely. But Patrick had become a slave to Christ, and the Lord gave him compassion for the Irish. "I was struck to the heart," he later wrote.

Patrick returned to primarily pagan Ireland, determined to bring the Gospel to people enslaved by superstition. Traveling throughout the land, he baptized thousands, discipled new believers, trained church leaders, ordained pastors, exerted discipline on unrepentant church members, and commissioned more evangelists. He started scores of churches and witnessed to kings and their courts, farmers and peasants. He also forcefully protested injustices against the common people. By the time he died, about 461 A.D., he had started a movement of the church that transformed ancient Ireland.

Through centuries God has raised up uniquely gifted evangelists to proclaim the truth to a lost world. That the calling of evangelist is a specific gift conferred by God has never been more evident than in the life of an upstate New York lawyer named Charles Finney. Converted to Christ in 1821 at age 29, Finney left his successful law practice to become a Presbyterian minister. He told his family and friends that he now had but one client, with "a retainer from the Lord Jesus Christ to plead His cause."[2]

As a result of Finney's preaching during the spring of 1824, a series of revivals broke out in that area and around the state, spreading to Philadelphia and Boston. Church congregations were set on fire, new churches formed.

The greatest evangelist of this century—perhaps the greatest since Paul—Billy Graham, has fervently, yet humbly preached the Gospel to over 100,000,000 people in 84 countries. Like Patrick, Finney and others, his influence results from the anointing of the Spirit and his single-minded devotion to his call from God.

I was among those who, a decade ago, urged Billy to give up strenuous crusades and spend more time writing and teaching. It's the only time I've ever seen him agitated.

"No," he said. "My call is to preach the Gospel, and I will do that as long as God gives me the breath to preach."

Graham has been equally unswerving in his commitment to the church, both to the unity of the whole body and to the local confessing congregations.

There are also people in the body of Christ who may not be called to full-time evangelism, but who are gifted in winning others to Christ. The late Arthur DeMoss, insurance company founder, was surely one.

When Art and his family traveled by air, they often did not sit together. Scattered through the plane, the children would witness to their seatmates. Art would engage anyone in conversation; and before long he would have shared his own testimony, often leading the person to Christ.

At Art's memorial service in 1979—one of the greatest celebrations I've ever witnessed—the pastor asked those who had come to Christ through Art's ministry to stand. Throughout that packed congregation, men and women rose to their feet. What a legacy!

But what about those who don't have a special gift and boldness for sharing the faith? Are we off the hook? No. For while God does specifically gift some for evangelism, all of us in the community of faith have a responsibility to bear the Good News. Even if we are uncomfortable doing it, we'd best obey when the Holy Spirit nudges us. I'm especially sensitve to this because that's how I came to Christ.

Whenever I tell the story of my conversion, I give my own perspective on how Tom Phillips told me about Christ. Only years later did I learn how Tom felt at the time.

Tom Phillips is a shrewd executive and a strong Christian. He is also one who feels awkward creating a scenario soley for the purpose of sharing his faith. It was unusual that he set his sights on me. Actually, he didn't want to. God just wouldn't let him off the hook.

In the Spring of 1973, Tom was president of Raytheon, one of America's largest and most successful companies. I had recently left the White House and planned to return to Raytheon as legal advisor. Tom was nervous about meeting with me because I was in the midst of the burgeoning Watergate controversy. That could hurt the company. Tom had changed a lot since he had become a Christian. We had known each other before on altogether different terms.

As he tells it, he asked God to "make Chuck Colson go away." He felt the Lord say to him, "No, you tell Chuck about me. He needs a friend."

Tom didn't want to tell me about Christ. But he was the one the Holy Spirit had tagged— and empowered—for that particular task. He was the one chosen to break my resistance.

We were both miserable. Yet it was God's appointed hour—and how eternally grateful I am for Tom Phillips' obedience.

In the Great Commission the verb tense Jesus used meant literally, *"as you are going* make disciples." *As you go.* Evangelism is not a set a of formulas, techniques, or memorized scenarios. It is a consequence of holy living, of our own personal passion for Christ, and naturally flows out of the healthy life of the church.

This is not a book about evangelism and we will not deal exhaustively with the subject. But if the church is to be effective in evangelizing today's world, there are a few critical concerns we should discuss. With opportunities to share our faith, we often face formidable barriers.

First, we must recognize that we live in a post-Christian culture.

During World War II, after Hitler blitzkrieged his way across France, demanding unconditional surrender from Allied forces in Europe, thousands of British and French troops dug in along the coast of northern France in a last-ditch effort to hold off the German forces. They knew they were trapped and would soon be obliterated by the Nazis.

As they waited, British soldiers reportedly broadcast a three-word message across the English Channel: "And if not."

"And if not"? Was it code?

No. It was a reference to the time Shadrach, Meshach, and Abednego faced King Nebuchadnezzar's fiery furnace. "Our God is able to save us, and He will save us," they said, *"and if not*, we will remain faithful to Him anyway." Believe it or not, the message was immediately understood.

In the following days, a rag-tag flotilla of boats set out from the shores of England and rescued 338,000 Allied troops.

If the same message came to America today, it would be greeted with raised eyebrows and blank stares—even from many Christians. We are no longer bound by common religious belief or heritage. The closest we come to a "connection" are the messages that flow from our television sets.

In the 1930s and 40s and into the 60s prefacing a statement with "The Bible says . . . " commanded respect. At that time 65 percent of all Americans believed the Bible to be literally true. Today only 32 percent actually believe the Bible is true.[3] So if you say, "the Bible says," only one out of three Americans may even listen.

As we discussed earlier, the prevailing world view denies the existence of absolute truth. So when the Christian message is proclaimed, modern listeners hear what they interpret as simply one person's preference—another autonomous human's choice of lifestyle or belief. *If Christianity works for you, that's great. But it doesn't mean much for me.* Thus, even your personal testimony may not necessarily be convicting.

I discovered this recently when talking with an acquaintance who happens to be a prominent journalist in New York. He was intrigued by my commitment to Jesus Christ, and we met for dinner to discuss it. When I started talking about what Christ had done in my life, he cut me off.

"It's wonderful that you've found peace and fulfillment through Jesus," he said in effect, "but I don't believe in Jesus." He told me he had friends in the New Age movement who had found spirituality too; it had worked for them as well as Christ had "worked" for me.

Then I began to talk about eternal life. Surely he had done some thinking about his own mortality. Again he cut me off. Death was simply the end, he said. And there was no such thing as an afterlife.

I talked about the Bible. "All legends," he interrupted.

What could I say? He didn't care about eternity or the Bible.

Perhaps it's when our canned answers don't work that God uses us most effectively. As I fumbled with my fork and my facts, an idea popped into my head.

"Have you seen Woody Allen's *Crimes and Misdemeanors*?" I asked.

He had, and we talked about it for a few minutes. Then, catching him off guard, I asked, "Are you Judah Rosenthal?"

He laughed—nervously.

"You may think this life is all there is," I said, "but if so, how do you live with yourself while you're here?"

He picked at his food and said that very issue gave him a lot of problems. Then somehow we moved into a discussion of Leo Tolstoy's novel, *War and Peace*, in which Pierre, the central character, cries out, "Why is it that I know what is right but do what is wrong?" That led us to C. S. Lewis's concept of the natural law ingrained in all of us, and then to the central point of Romans 1: that we all are imbued with a conscience, run from it though we might, and that it points to questions which can only be answered outside of ourselves.

I don't know what's going to happen to this friend. My hunch is he will come to Christ, because I believe the Holy Spirit is hounding him. But I know one thing: without Woody Allen, Leo Tolstoy, and C. S. Lewis, we wouldn't have had the common ground on which to discuss the spiritual realm.

This tells us that to evangelize today we must address the human condition at its point of felt need—conscience, guilt, dealing with others, finding a purpose for staying alive. Talking about the abundant life or life everlasting or Bible promises often just won't do it.

The knowledge of God is in each of us, and through the power of the Holy Spirit the Word of God can penetrate the toughest human heart. We are not suggesting that we cannot present the truth directly and frontally to our listeners, nor that we should not share our testimonies; of course we should, and God will often use them to convict others.

> *The knowledge of God is in each of us, and through the power of the Holy Spirit the Word of God can penetrate the toughest human heart.*

But on a purely rational level, apart from the benediction of the Holy Spirit, the secular person's existential mindset precludes their understanding us. As George Hunter, dean at Asbury Seminary, has argued, we are similar to the first-century church; we need to educate in order to witness.

We must be familiar enough with the prevailing world view to look for points of contact and discern points of disagreement. This is a tremendous challenge to the church, and particularly to evangelicals. Almost all of our evangelistic motives and methods were developed in the 1940s and 1950s, some in the 1960s, when Christian presuppositions were commonly understood, when two-thirds of the people believed the Bible. Today all that has changed. So we must examine and perhaps drastically overhaul our motives and methods to engage the modern mind.

Our prepackaged "God-talk" won't do. Before we tell people what the Bible says, we have to tell them why they should believe it. And we need a Christian apologetic that touches chords within our unbelieving friends and begins to alter their view of reality.

This leads to a second point. To reach the modern world demands both sensitivity and creativity.

Odessa Moore, a Prison Fellowship volunteer and member of the Faithful Central Missionary Baptist Church in south-central Los Angeles, is a good example.

Eight years ago she visited the juvenile jail and met a teenager waiting to be tried as an adult for first-degree murder. His eyes chilled her, they were so full of hatred and anger.

"I don't care about anything," he said defiantly. "I don't feel no shame."

A familiar story emerged as they talked—father a drug user, mother an alcoholic, both parents abusive. They would beat the boy and tie him up in the closet for hours. All of his life he had been told he was nothing. No one cared about him. But that was all right, he said.

"I don't care about nobody."

"There is someone who loves you," Odessa told him.

"No way," he responded. "Nobody."

"You're in here for murder, right?" asked Odessa.

"Yes, and I'd do it again," he said.

"If someone came in here tonight and said, 'I know you committed the murder, and they are going to give you the death penalty, but I am going to take your place for you.' How would you like that?"

For the first time the boy showed a spark of life. "That would be great!"

Odessa went on to tell him about Jesus, the Prisoner who did take his place, who had already paid the price for his wrongdoing. Using word pictures the young man could understand, she walked him through the steps to a growing understanding of sin, repentance, forgiveness, and true freedom in Christ.

By the end of the evening the stone-cold teenager had melted, weeping tears of repentance and committed his life to Christ.

I have experienced this on hundreds of occasions. Christianity seems remote to prisoners; but when I talk about the historic Jesus who was executed for a crime He didn't commit, their eyes light up. This they can relate to.

Many churches are doing this same kind of "translating" in their communities. Perhaps the best-known example is Willow Creek in South Barrington, Illinois.

In the summer of 1975 seminary student Bill Hybels and a couple of his buddies conducted a door-to-door survey throughout the west Chicago suburbs. They simply asked, "Do you regularly attend a local church?" If the answer was yes, they thanked the respondent and moved on. If it was no, they asked the follow-up, "Why not?"

They got an earful. But essentially there were four reasons people did not attend church:

1. Churches are always asking for money.

2. Church services are boring and predictable.

3. Church is irrelevant to real life.

4. Pastors make people feel ignorant and guilty.

Targeting the huge population of unchurched baby boomers in those Chicago suburbs, Hybels and his colleagues began a church that would, while faithfully preaching the Gospel, address these four objections. They also listened carefully to the people who came, discovering their expressed needs and discerning the unexpressed, and they designed a church experience that would feel comfortable but also intrigue and challenge: "a safe place to hear a dangerous sermon!" The new local body, meeting in a movie theater, began to grow.

By the early 1990s, 14,000 a week were gathering at Willow Creek. But not just on Sunday morning. The facilities hum with activities all week, from the weekend "seeker services" on Saturday evenings and Sunday mornings, designed to draw in unbelievers, to the midweek worship services on Wednesday and Thursday evenings, designed for believers to grow deeper in their faith.

Willow Creek isn't for everyone nor does it claim to be. And, like all churches, it has its warts. It's been accused by some of bending the Gospel and being too market-oriented. But Willow Creek strives to keep its purpose clear.

"We believe in the fundamentals of Scripture . . . and we don't want to mess with them at all. But we want to translate them for the society we live in," says Mark Mittelberg.

And what that means, adds Lee Strobel, once legal affairs editor of the *Chicago Tribune*, "is that we're not just using entertainment to pacify people, or help them have fun. We are taking contemporary art forms—music, drama, dance, multi-media, video—to communicate Christ. We take the historic Christian message and translate it into language twentieth-century Americans understand; in that way, a suburbanite like me, a cynic, can come in and be hit right in the heart with the Gospel."

> *When evangelism is based on the biblical model, it naturally follows worship and fellowship and leads to discipleship.*

Willow Creek is only one of hundreds of churches consciously endeavoring to evangelize in ways modern men and women can understand. But its fervor for evangelism doesn't blind this local body to its proper priorities, as its objectives clearly show:

1. To exalt God in worship.

2. To evangelize, bringing people to a saving knowledge of Christ, with a church attitude that is outward oriented rather than a holy huddle mentality.

3. To edify, taking new Christians and maturing them in the faith.

4. To extend, reaching out into the community to meet physical, spiritual, relational, and emotional needs.

Right priorities lead us directly to the third point about evangelism, that it flows out of worship.

When evangelism is based on the biblical model, it naturally follows worship and fellowship and leads to discipleship; it is a byproduct of spiritual life flowing from a healthy body being nourished by the Head. For this reason, the worship service itself should not be primarily evangelistic.

Which leads to the fourth point. Evangelism should always be designed to bring the convert into the local church, where the work of discipleship can be done.

Evangelicals are forever organizing highly publicized campaigns to win people to Christ. We pick up some catchy name, "mission this or mission that," raise money on the promise of a new Great Awakening, barrage some area or group, count the hands raised—which, particularly overseas, may be nothing more than a polite response—and then boast about the number of decisions.

I've become so dismayed with this kind of scalp-hunting that I will not give an invitation unless I know in advance there is a follow-up mechanism in place. It is a gross disservice to unsaved people—and an impediment to the cause of Christ to get them excited, lead them into some emotional response, and then dump them on the doorstep. Unless evangelism brings converts into the visible body of Christ, it is like assisting at a baby's birth and then leaving the infant out in the cold alone.

When evangelistic efforts are not integrated with the local church, they run the grave danger of being out of the will of God. The Great Commission by definition involves baptism and disciple-making, which can only be done within a local confessing congregation. Regardless of how and where a person comes to know Christ, it must be a normative practice to immediately bring him into the fellowship and discipline of a *local* church.

J. C. Harris, pastor of a Baptist church and chaplain in a North Carolina prison, has taken pains to do the same. In the prison he constantly seeks to bring inmates to Christ. But when a prisoner does make a profession of faith, J. C. counsels the new convert about choosing and joining a local church in his hometown—even though he's still in prison.

> *The church needs to understand that its mission is not just to get people through the doors and onto membership rolls and call this evangelism, but also to make disciples.*

"We don't baptize people," he says. "Baptism is an ordinance of the church. We want our men baptized into the fellowship of a church in their hometown, and then to become a long-distance part of that particular congregation, just as if they were away in the Army or something. Then, when they get out, they go back home and their church families are waiting for them, ready to help with clothes, food, a job—and accountability."

One of Billy Graham's biographers wrote important words: "the true object of evangelism, in the context of the Great Commission, is discipleship." But the church needs to understand that its mission is not just to get people through the doors and onto membership rolls and call this evangelism, but also to make disciples.

Which leads to our fifth point. Evangelism is to be directed at the non-Christian.

Sounds obvious, but surveys show that as much as 85 percent of church membership growth is made up of people who church-hop. Other surveys show that there has been no real growth in church membership in recent years; increase in some denominations is simply offset by decrease in others. We cannot compete with neighboring churches or scoop up the church shoppers and then boast about successful evangelism. Evangelism is for the unsaved.

Churches across the country are doing this in thousands of creative ways. Consider just a few examples:

The Whittier Area Baptist Fellowship in Southern California sponsors quarterly "Teddy Bear

Parties," where three and four-year-olds from the neighborhood are invited to bring their favorite stuffed bear to a church tea party. Their mothers come too and, in the process, learn about the church's children's programs and other ministries.

During the Christmas season each year, McLean Presbyterian Church, just outside of Washington, D.C., hosts evangelistic teas. These small gatherings of neighbors, hosted by a church member, offer morning coffee and Christmas goodies and a refreshing pause in the Christmas rush. The hostess asks everyone to share a special Christmas memory or family tradition; then a lay speaker from the church gives a short talk about the Christ whose arrival Christmas celebrates.

At the St. Stephens church of God in Christ in San Diego, California, evangelistic teams called "block-busters" hit the streets of their drug-ridden inner-city neighborhood on Friday evenings. For the groups of young people loitering on the street corners smoking pot, drinking beer, and killing time, the block-busters are a diversion. They talk to the kids one-on-one and give them appropriately designed tracts they can read later.

Most importantly, a number of the block-busters are living tracts: they themselves have been delivered from drugs, hopelessness, and a life without Christ. Over the past fourteen years many young people have come to Christ, been discipled in the church, and gone back out to the streets to bring in their peers.

Southeast Christian Church in Louisville, Kentucky, sponsors a yearly outreach to the community called the "Drug House Odyssey," a full-scale dramatic event. The production begins with a depiction of a drug deal, and then shows a drug bust. The drama then moves to a courtroom scene and concludes in a penitentiary. Afterward, police officers and church members are standing by to answer questions and pass out literature.

The church has been entrusted with truth and hope in an age that knows neither.

First-century believers, when challenged or told to cease proclaiming the Good News by the authorities of the day, burst out, "We cannot stop talking about what we have seen and heard."

In the same way, modern-day evangelism must exuberantly flow from our character as a worshiping, godly community; it must be done in the context of the corporate body and must articulate the Gospel in language twentieth-century men and women can understand.

But as we said at the outset of this chapter, we will not always *proclaim* the Gospel. Sometimes, in order to be heard, we must first be *seen*. We must *be* the Gospel!

Lights shining out in the darkness, like candles that illuminate and warm and draw others toward the one true light.

NOTES

1. Sheldon Van Auken, *A Severe Mercy* (New York: Bantam, 1977), 82.

2. Garth Rosell, "Charles Gradison Finney," *Great Leaders of the Christian Church*, John D. Woodbridge, ed. (Chicago : Moody Press, 1988), 318.

3.   From Ellen Vaughn interviews at Willow Creek, 24
      August 1991.

Portions of this chapter have been adapted from a chapter in
The Body by Chuck Colson: Copyright 1993 by Word, Inc.,
Dallas, Texas. Used by permission.

■ GROWTH STRATEGIES ■

1. What can you learn about evangelism
    from the following passages?

    Matthew 28:19–20

    Luke 24:27

2. What is the difference between "being" a
    witness and "proclaiming" a witness?
    How can you develop a lifestyle of "being"
    a witness?

3. Do you sometimes feel hesitant about
    sharing Christ? How can you become
    more comfortable?

4. How would you respond to my friend who
    said, "It's wonderful that you've found
    peace and fulfillment through Jesus, but I
    don't believe in Jesus?"

5. What role does the local church play in
    evangelism?

CHAPTER 15

VALUES/SERVICE

Dr. Tony Campolo
Pastor, Speaker, Author
Chairman, Sociology Department, Eastern College

■ CHAPTER OBJECTIVE ■

This chapter is about having fun. There isn't anything frivolous about having fun. Learning how to have fun is one of the most serious subjects in the world.

Without fun, marriages don't work. When jobs aren't fun, they become intolerable and dehumanizing. When children aren't fun, they are heartbreaking. When church is not fun, religion becomes a drag. When life is not fun, it is hard to be spiritual.

People don't know how to have fun. They force themselves to do things that are supposed to be fun, but frequently they end up with a hollow feeling instead of the euphoria they expected to experience. They put on the faces of happiness as they consciously present themselves to one another at cocktail parties; yet, in unguarded, pensive moments, their faces sag and their expressions spell deadness and ennui. When you ask them how things are going, they say, "Couldn't be better." But you sense that perhaps they couldn't be worse.

Once when I was at Disneyland, I saw a woman shaking her little boy and screaming at him, "You wanted to come, and now you're going to have fun whether you like it or not!" It seems to me that too many people are just like that little boy. They are supposed to be having fun, but they feel like crying. It does no good for them to force themselves to have fun. Having fun can't be forced, but it can be learned.

> *If we want to get the most out of life, we must learn to give priority to those things that are really important.*

Too often, we miss out on the best that life has to offer because we are distracted by what is of little consequence while ignoring that which is most deserving of our time and energy. All too easily we get our value systems mixed up and then become confused about what delivers the fun that God wants us to enjoy.

THE WAY THINGS LOOK TODAY

On April 7, 1980, *Fortune* magazine carried an article titled "On a Fast Track to the Good Life." The article gave the findings of research done to clarify the values and attitudes of twenty-five-year-olds who were taking their places in the business world of the 1980s. The research was intended to give the readers of *Fortune* a thumbnail sketch of what to expect from young people during the next ten years. The study was most revealing. Allow me to introduce you to that generation of twenty-year-olds, but don't be surprised if they sound strikingly familiar.

1. These young people believed that a successful life meant financial independence and that the best way to gain financial independence was to be at the top of a major corporation.

2. They believed in themselves. They believed that they had the abilities and capacities to be the best. There was no "humble talk" among them.

3. They believed in the corporate world. They were sure that the corporations they would lead would be the most worthwhile institutions in the world.

4. They viewed as "a drag on success" any relationship that slowed their ascent of the corporate ladder. Marriage was an acceptable option only if it didn't interfere with their aspirations for success. Having children, for most of them, was something to which they would have to give a great deal of thought.

5. Loyalty was not high on their list of values. Unlike "The Organization Man," described by William Whyte, Jr., in his book by the same title during the 1950s, the young Turks of this new breed had their resumes ever at hand. They were ready to move from one company to another and believed that loyalty to one company could lead to staying in a system that might not maximize upward mobility.

6. They were convinced that they were more creative and imaginative than those who then held top corporate positions, and they believed that there wasn't much they

could learn from those older types before they took their places.

When I read about these young people and their values, I felt sad and deeply troubled. I think Jesus would have said to them, "For what will a profit a man if he gains the whole world, and loses his own soul?" (Mark 8:36). After reading the Fortune article, I was left with a sense that this new generation of young people would find most of the teachings of Jesus incomprehensible and that what they did understand, they would deem unacceptable.

WHAT JESUS TAUGHT

The Beatitudes, as outlined in Matthew 5, are the antitheses of what those young people were all about. Jesus contended that those who become poor as they respond to the needs of others will be the happiest of people. But the "yuppies," the upwardly mobile young professionals of the 1980s, argued that happiness results from gaining financial success for self.

Jesus taught that those who are the happiest are those who are able to empathize with the sufferings of others. Students coming out of college these days tend to believe that happiness can best be found by focusing on their own well-being and not worrying about what breaks the hearts of those outside their personal worlds.

Whereas Jesus called meek people happy (Matt. 5:5), most young, upwardly mobile professionals believe that happiness comes through a go-getting, success-seeking attitude that leaves little room for loyalty to others.

Jesus' teaching about purity of heart (Matt. 5:8) must seem hopelessly naive to the youth of the 1980s. They believe that everybody is out for "number one" and that behind even the most altruistic behavior are motives that are oriented to personal gratification and sexual pleasure.

Their commitment to success at all costs makes them somewhat merciless towards those whose personal limitations prevent them from gaining a share in the American dream. They believe that people get what they deserve, and those who fall by the wayside warrant little attention from those who have the talent and make the sacrifices essential for personal achievement. What Jesus says about being merciful (Matt. 5:7) must seem to them like shallow and ineffective sentimentalism. Jesus told us that peacemaking brings happiness (Matt. 5:9), but they are too committed to aggressively displacing their corporate superiors to pay much attention to such a thought. They believe in that Spencerian doctrine that the world is basically a jungle and only those who have the instinct to compete for survival are able to live in it.

The yuppie generation is interested in having good reports on their accomplishments. They want their resumes and their letters of recommendation to strengthen their position in the job market. They are not willing to be "persecuted for righteousness' sake" (Matt. 5:10). The idea of taking unpopular stands and opposing practices that reek of injustice seems foolhardy when such stands may elicit negative responses from those in positions of power and influence.

They go to church, but these contemporary yuppies are hardly the possessors of a Christian value system. Their successes may be a source of pride to their parents, but there is an anxiety among these parents that is not pleasant to behold. They repress a fear that when they are old, they will not be visited or tended to with much love by these upwardly mobile, tough-minded children.

I have been writing "they" consistently on the last several pages while fully aware that I could have written "you." This choice was not a hesitation to be direct on my part. Rather, I wanted to give you a chance to reflect objectively on your own generation. I wanted you to feel the size of the task ahead of you when you take the call to follow Christ seriously. A lot of changes will have to occur on the way to having fun!

SOME WORDS FROM THE WISE

Recently, I read a sociological study that has great significance for those of us who are trying to respond to champions of the yuppie value system. In this particular study, fifty people over the age of ninety-five were asked one question: "If you could live your life over again, what would you do differently?" It was an open-ended question to which these elderly responded in a variety of ways. Three specific answers, however, constantly emerged and dominated the results of the study. These three answers were:

1. If I had it to do over again, I would *reflect more.*

2. If I had it to do over again, I would *risk more.*

3. If I had it to do over again, I would *do more things that would live on after I am dead.*

I think these elderly people have a good handle on what life is all about. I believe their perspective gives better direction on how to live life with joy and satisfaction than we can gain from listening to the current wisdom on the way to live. So, I want to look briefly at each of those statements. I am convinced that people who want to have fun in life would do well to consider the observations of those whom time has made wise.

REFLECTING: GIVING MORE THOUGHT TO LIFE

The elderly people in the study realized in retrospect that they had not paid proper attention to the things in life that were of the greatest importance. They recognized that they had failed to appreciate properly many of the blessings that had been theirs by the grace of God. They sensed that they had not paid enough attention to the people who had been a major part of their lives. In short, they realized that they had not experienced life and all that it had to offer them with the depth and gratitude it deserved. Life had happened around them while they had been busy doing everything else.

Here are a few of those important things upon which it is worth reflecting regularly:

Grace of God

Even new Christians can easily explain what Jesus did for us on the cross. With relative ease, we can declare that the Son of God was put to death because of our sins. All too casually, we can point out that each of us is deserving of punishment from God, but that Jesus was punished in our place. We can give both the long and the short versions of what happened on the cross. But our words are full of explanations that sound rehearsed while lacking in exclamations that come from wonder. We verbalize reasons for the cross while failing to reflect upon what Jesus suffered on our behalf.

> *I am convinced that if we reflected more about the pain and agony our sins brought upon Jesus two thousand years ago, our lives would be completely different.*

God's Glory

Sometimes, when life is overbearing, one of the few routes to joy we can find is in thinking about our new standing before God because of Christ. Sometimes, when people around us make us feel like nothing, the best therapy we can find is in reflecting about how God sees us and what He has declared us to be before the angels in glory. The Bible teaches us that God views us through His Son. Not only does Jesus take our sin and make it His own, but He ascribes to us all the benefits for the good things that He has done, is doing, and will do. When I reflect on this, I often experience a psychic "high."

I don't have to be afraid on Judgment Day, because all my sins are forgiven and forgotten. They are blotted out and remembered no more. When my heavenly Father opens the Campolo book and reads about me, I haven't a thing to worry about. All the things in my life that are rotten and filthy, and all the things that are so shameful that I have never dared to share them with anyone, will be erased from my records. In place of all that garbage will be recorded all the magnificent things that Jesus did. That's incredibly good news. Heaven is going to be fun! It's even fun to anticipate the experience!

The joy that comes from thinking about glory is a joy available to all who have surrendered their lives to Christ. All they have to do is just stop and reflect on it all from time to time.

Relationships

Think of it: life is a complex chain of relationships. The wise elders in this study learned that the precious times we have with each other slip quickly by without our giving them the intensive attention they deserve. They could nod in painful agreement to the central question directed to the audience in the familiar play *Our Town*, "Do any of you ever really live life while you're living it?" I am over fifty years old. Both my son and my daughter are grown up and out of the house. I know that, for the most part, they are out of my everyday life, and I will never again see as much of them as I would like. But in my quiet times, I can recall those special moments when I stopped and allowed myself to feel their preciousness. I wish I had done more such reflecting. I wish I had taken less for granted during our precious times together.

RISK-TAKING: THE STUFF THAT HEROES ARE MADE OF

Risk-taking is exciting. Risk-taking makes you feel heroic. Risk-taking gives you evidence that you are special. Risk-taking convinces you that you've got what it takes to break out of the mold that society casts for you. It is no wonder, then, that the elderly people surveyed in the study claimed that, if they had life to live over again, they would risk more.

Looking back on life, these people didn't think much about their successes nor did they show much remorse over their failures. From the vantage point of old age, life's successes did not seem like such a big deal and life's failures did not appear to be the disasters they thought they were at the time they were happening. To people who were ninety-five years of age and older, what seemed to matter were the risks they had taken, what they had been bold enough to try!

There are people who have jobs that make them miserable but who won't quit because they are afraid of the risk. Each morning, they make themselves go to jobs they hate and endure humiliation from bosses they don't like, all because they cannot bring themselves to risk their limited security. These suffering people live out their lives in quiet desperation, knowing neither the thrill of victory nor the

agony of defeat. They survive by detaching
themselves from what they do and fantasizing
about being in other places, doing other things.
They become absent when they are present.
The joy goes out of their lives, and being with
them is no longer fun. It's not that they don't
realize what's happening. They do. They can
sense themselves dying in their jobs, but they
haven't got what it takes to launch out into
something dangerously new and different.

> *The Promised Land belongs to the person*
> *who takes the risks, whose face is marred*
> *by dust and sweat, who strives valiantly*
> *while daring everything.*

It is true that there are great possibilities for
failure in risk-taking. And if you fail, there will
be those who will mock you. But mockers are
not important. Those who like to point when
the risk-takers stumble don't count. The criticisms of those who sit back, observe, and offer
smug suggestions can be discounted. The Promised Land belongs to the person who takes the
risks, whose face is marred by dust and sweat,
who strives valiantly while daring everything,
who may err and fall, but who has done his or
her best. This person's place shall never be
with those cold and timid souls who know neither victory nor defeat.

Oh, if only I could persuade timid souls I meet
to listen to that inner voice of the Spirit that
challenges us to attempt great things for God
and expect great things from God. Oh, if only I
could inspire them to heed that inner urging
that tells them, "Go for it!" I cannot say what a

person should do with life, but I can say what a person should not do with it. No one should devote one's life to safety, to a course of action that offers no challenge and no fun.

I wonder how many of those reading this book have thought about going to the mission field, or maybe considered undertaking some daring work for Christ, right here, on the home front, but have backed off because of fear of the risks. Perhaps you've been thinking about leaving a job that isn't giving you much fulfillment and doing something heroic for Christ and His kingdom, but you don't seem to be able to bring yourself to the point where you can "lay aside every weight, and the sin which so easily ensnares us, and let us run with endurance the race that is set before us" (Heb 12:1). My advice is to pray long and hard. Get Christian friends to pray with you, and then "go for it."

DOING THINGS THAT LAST

Let's return to the study of the fifty elderly subjects who were asked what they would have done differently if they had life to live over again. "We would have done more things that would live on after we are dead," they said.

There is a latent desire in every human being to do something of worth that will have lasting significance. There is a longing in most people to do something that will make life better for others. When we confront the reality of death, we become fully aware of the importance of leaving something good behind. That is why young people give little thought to the significance of their lives, while the elderly think about it all the time. In the face of the end of life, questions about its significance loom large. Many who have been blasè about the meaning of life approach death fearing that their epitaph will read like that on the tomb of the poet Keats: "Here lies one whose name is writ in water."

ANOTHER WAY

Each year we have a student recognition day at our church. On the Sunday between Christmas and New Year's Day, we ask the young people of our church who are students at colleges and universities to give us reports of how their educational experiences have been going. It is a very special Sunday because ours is a black Baptist church. The older members of our congregation have not had the educational opportunities that our young people enjoy. Consequently, they love to hear about what their children and grandchildren are learning.

On one such Sunday, after half a dozen students had given their reports, my pastor got up and delivered some closing words. "Children," he said, "you're going to die! You may not think you're going to die. But you're going to die. One of these days, they're going to take you out to the cemetery, drop you in a hole, throw some dirt on your face, and go back to the church and eat potato salad.

"When you were born," he said, "you alone were crying and everybody else was happy. The important question I want to ask is this: When you die are you alone going to be happy, leaving everybody else crying? The answer depends on whether you live to get titles or you live to get testimonies. When they lay you in the grave, are people going to stand around reciting fancy titles you earned, or are they going to stand around giving testimonies of the good things you did for them? Will they list your degrees and awards, or will they tell about what a blessing you were to them? Will you leave behind just a newspaper column telling people how important you were, or will you leave crying people who give testimonies of how they've lost the best friend they ever had? There's nothing wrong with titles. Titles are good things to have. But if it ever comes down to a choice between a title or a testimony—go for the testimony."

At this point, my pastor was only getting warmed up. He proceeded to take us through the Bible, forcefully pointing out the contrasts between people who had titles—like Pharaoh, Nebuchadnezzar, Queen Jezebel, and Pilate—and those who left behind glorious testimonies—like Moses, Daniel, Elijah, and Jesus.

The old people whose values we are considering would have said a hearty "Amen!" to my pastor's message. They would have agreed that testimonies are more important than titles. They would have agreed that those things we do for others will be remembered after we are gone. Those are the things that should be our top priority.

BACK TO GETTING THE MOST OUT OF LIFE

The fact is that many of us do not know how to have fun. How can we, when we do not even know what is important or what delivers a fun time? How can any of us have a good time in life when we ignore the things God has designed to deliver His joy? How can we know happiness if we give our lives to the things He warned would only make us sad?

If we are to be fun people, we must get our values clarified. We must put first things first. We must give attention to those things that foster good family life, satisfying work patterns, positive church life, and viable church relationships. We must give our time and energy to those things that God teaches us to value, and construct our styles so that we organize our lives around those things essential to life as He wills it to be lived. In other words, if we are to get the most out of life, and have fun doing it, we have to get our values straightened out. It will take reflection. There will be risks. But our aim will be to go for things that really last, that are eternal!

Adapted from *Who Switched The Price Tags?* by Anthony Campolo; published by WORD, Dallas Texas, 1986. Used by permission.

■ GROWTH STRATEGIES ■

1. In each of these passages, what was Jesus
    teaching about how we should live?

    Matthew 5:5

    Matthew 5:7

    Matthew 5:8

    Matthew 5:9

    Matthew 5:10

2. How do the values taught by Christ
    contrast with the values commonly held in
    our world?

3. How do most men in our society find
    meaning and purpose for their lives?

4. What gives your life significance?

5. How can you spend more time reflecting
    on God's grace, glory, and your
    relationship with Him?

6. Where do you need to take more risks?

7. What should you spend less time on (things that will not last)? What should you spend more time on (things that will last)?

CHAPTER 16

CHRISTIAN STEWARDSHIP

Fred Smith
Speaker, author, and business consultant

■ CHAPTER OBJECTIVE ■

Most of us think of stewardship and money as
synonymous. They aren't. There are good stew-
ards of money who are poor stewards of life.
First I want to talk about life, and then we'll
talk about money.

THE STEWARDSHIP OF IDENTITY

Ray Stedman, in his excellent series *A Pilgrim's Life in an Alien World*, said, "I was struck, in reading Michael Green's book *Evangelism in the Early Church* by the fact that Christians in the first century influenced their world for Jesus Christ far more than Christians do in our day. Their world was more openly hostile to Christianity than ours, they were far fewer in number, they did not hold any influential positions, they did not have our money or our technology. Yet in a span of thirty years, they succeeded in spreading the Kingdom of God from Jerusalem to Antioch to Corinth to Ephesus and then to the capital of the Roman Empire itself. Christians today have more established rights; they are greater in number; they are more influential; they hold some of the most influential positions in the land; they have all the money and technology they need. Yet their influence in the world seems stifled and anemic by comparison." He goes on to say that he believes their strength was in their identity. They were "sojourners." And while we are American Christians, they were pilgrims, citizens of heaven, on their way home. The reality of eternity is the ultimate orifice through which all of our thinking must be channeled in order to be effective. The more we become conscious of eternity, the more nearly Christian we become.

The pastor of a large Baptist church in Moscow said he had 5,600 members. I asked, "How many attend?" and he said, "6,000." I told him this was a little different ratio than we have here in Texas. He said, yes, they had about 400 who were not ready yet to take the identity of Christian, but they did attend. And then he used a very interesting phrase. He said, "In Russia we have no four-wheel Christians"—those who ride to their baptism, ride to Easter, ride to Christmas service, and ride to their funeral.

I began to think of Christians who divide into participants and observers. I once asked one of the finest secular scholars in America what he thought the most important question is, and he said, "The next question." Then I realized that he was more an intellectual reporter on life than a participant. I can't fault him, for this is also often my biography.

I have never felt that evangelism is my gift. I have found this interesting possibility, however. Each morning, I tell the Lord, "Today I won't duck." In other words, if religion comes up in a natural way in a conversation, I will deal with it just as I would any other subject, including sex or inflation. I have been surprised how often, when I pray that, in some way somebody will mention the subject of religion, and I will become involved.

I have a colorful three-inch round pin that an advertising executive in Fresno made for the men of his church in their annual retreat after I had told my experience with "no ducking." It's a picture of a duck in a large circle with a black line drawn through it—a pictorial message for "no ducking." He gave out 125 of these to the men attending. I think of this as stewardship of identity.

I have found that if I duck natural conversations about spiritual matters, I can't make up for it by formal church visitation programs.

Being identified as a Christian is a responsibility. For example, I personally do not feel obligated to pray over my food in public places, but I am delighted to share where the prayer is sincere and not for show. I think the Bible teaches that we should not pray to be seen of men. However, when we do pray over the food, I feel obligated to leave a larger tip than normal. I don't want the waitress looking down on "those cheap Christians." We have an identity to protect.

Certainly Christians should not lose the spontaneity of their love and appreciation for Christ. If a person is gregarious and uninhibited, then a word about Christ is very appropriate. There are others for whom this would be forced. For example, I met the president of a firm who said he felt he had to "drag Jesus into every conversation." That would not be natural or normal for me. I respect this man, but I don't feel I must imitate him. I prefer to depend more on the Spirit than on a routine or habit. Neither way is exclusively right or wrong. I do believe our witness of identity works best when it is real.

Sometimes your witness for Christ may only be a comment or an attitude, almost like a seed. Who knows? That might be the seed that, dropped in the crack of the rock, will one day split it. As Gert Behanna said, "What I need is not a psychiatrist, but God."

> *All of God's seeds are not perennial; some of them are like cactuses blooming only after a long gestation.*

When Orel Hersheiser quietly dropped to his knees in the play-offs, I turned to my wife, not knowing anything about the man, and said, "That was sincere." Later I met his pastor, Paul Cedar, who told me of the man's deep dedication to his Christian faith. He wasn't making a spectacle; he simply had to express his appreciation to the source of his strength and confirm his Christian identity.

THE STEWARDSHIP OF RELATIONS

Early Christians were known for their relationships with each other: "How they loved one another." They were not known for how the church grew, not even for a balanced budget. I have long felt that any success Christians claim which can be stated numerically is nonscriptural. Yet we have borrowed from business the language of numbers, because it is so easy to define success by figures and so difficult to define it by relationship. I can take an inventory of your money, your wealth, and give you a precise figure. I cannot take an inventory of your relationship with your wife and state it in numerical terms. Did you ever hear anybody say, "We have a marriage that I would rate about 76 percent?" Once I was foolish enough to try to put a numerical rating on the morale in our plants, particularly our non-union plants. We soon gave this up as totally impractical. We have to use terms like healthy, unhealthy, improving, or deteriorating. And I think in the church we should use the adjective scriptural.

The church is more like a family than a business—relationships are more important than numbers. The love defined by C.S. Lewis, "Willing the ultimate good for the other person," produces the atmosphere and the relationship the world can see and define as a genuine love.

A top executive of one of the large oil companies came on a weekend to talk to me about a merger they were considering. I hesitated to have him in my home because of his profanity. But after two days, as we returned to the airport, I could not remember his saying one offensive word; and our family had continued to have our Bible reading and prayer at the table, holding hands as always, while he was there. As we drove to the airport he said, "Fred, you haven't changed me, but thank you for not letting me change you all." Years later he dropped by a laymen's meeting where we were holding the Laymen's Institute. The next day he found me and told me he wanted to become a Christian because all his life he had dropped by churches from time to time trying to find the warmth and the spirit that he found the night before, and he wanted to be part of that.

When in Rome visiting the Catacombs, my guide was a wonderful English priest. As we came out, I wanted to mildly shock him so I said, "Father, I'm a Southern Baptist." He brightened up, slapped his hands together, and said, "Pep me up, brother, pep me up!" He had heard about us Baptists.

Then I said, "Father, I enjoyed the tour; and as we were going through the Catacombs, it occurred to me that those early Christians couldn't afford the luxury of denominational life."

Taking my shoulders between his hands he replied, "My brother, it is not the form that separates us but the blessed hope of the Resurrection which unites us." I fully expect to spend some time in heaven talking again with that priest who shared the hope of the Resurrection in the spirit of peacemaking.

> *As part of our stewardship of relations, we owe each other encouragement.*

There's enough pressure and tension today without us loading on unnecessary guilt and criticism of each other. I like the kind of encouragement that the president of a scientific laboratory gave to the medical convention when he said, "Gentlemen, my father was a country doctor, and we now know scientifically there wasn't a thing he carried in that black bag that would cure anybody. But people got well because he patted them and said, 'You're going to get well.'" That encouragement released the magnificent and amazing power of the body to heal itself.

Sometime I would love to participate in a serious study of the proper relation between Christian positivism and the healing process. Once we get the necessity of spiritual rebirth established, then we need to go on to the unlimited mysteries of abundant living that are available to us.

Our family relations are probably the most telling of our relational stewardship. It is difficult to be a Christian at home—not impossible, just difficult. Therefore, we have to work at it more conscientiously, because many of us are more interested in production than relation. We carry our office discipline into the home. We are executives in the office and executives at home. I made that mistake for many years. Our son made a difference in my life when he said, "Dad, relations are the production of a home."

One of my friends told me that if he had been a father at home instead of an executive, his marriage would still be together and his oldest son would still be alive. His wife had rebelled at the mechanical way he ran the home. Finally she couldn't take it any more, and so she left with the children. The son was driving to see his father when he was killed in an automobile accident.

While having lunch with seventeen prominent preachers, one of them said, "My brethren, I am weary of celebrity religion. I have had my share of celebrity treatment. But if when I die, my family members do not say, 'There is something of God in the man,' then I have failed." It brought the group to complete silence and contemplation. Our family must believe in us even if they themselves do not believe in Christ.

Not only are we responsible for "internal" relation stewardship with fellow Christians, we also have an "external" one with our peers. I associate with many who are quite moral without being Christians. Some of the men practice Christian ethics but make no claim to having the Christian experience.

The verse that comes to me in relation to our peers is that we are not to conform but to be transformed (Rom. 12:2). This means that we do not let the pressure from the outside determine who we are. Instead, the power from within is our determination. Here we think of salt, which not only preserves but improves the taste. We as Christians are in the business of redeeming situations and bringing taste to life.

The other metaphor is light, and its chief function is that we are able to see clearly. There should be a special clarity of judgment among Christians because they have light. We know that light is always taken to darkness rather than darkness to light. Our stewardship of relations touches our world redemptively.

THE STEWARDSHIP OF TALENTS/GIFTS

Generally, Christians talk much more about talents than about gifts. I have become more and more convinced that the gifts are what the

Spirit uses. I know that my dear friends who are theologians may differ with me on my interpretation of gifts, but they would be broad-minded enough to let me have my opinion even though it might be wrong. I firmly believe that gifts are talents that have been "unctionized" by the Spirit. "Unctionize" is my word for "blessed and empowered."

> *Unfortunately, we often try to use our human talents to do God's work.*

A person may sing with a beautiful voice but break the spirit of the service because he or she is utilizing a human talent and self-confidence rather than a dedicated spiritual gift. On the other hand, a person of much less talent blesses you because he or she sings with the gift of the Spirit.

All of us have potential gifts because all of us have talents that can be dedicated and unctionized. I list only a few, because we have limited space:

Teaching

Jim Smith, of Highland Park Presbyterian Church (Dallas), taught a class whose attendance went from 50 to 650. He did this not by contests but with content. When a teacher gives people what they desperately need and are looking for, I believe their ministry expands naturally. When we reach hungry people with real bread, they form a line.

Bill Glass, the former All-American defensive end, visited me this week. He calls me his "mentor" from the time we met when he was a student at Baylor. Through the years we have spent a great deal of time thinking together, but I assured him that while teaching might be one of my gifts, it was brought out only in the presence of a good student. The student makes the teacher; for without serious students, a teacher is only a monologist.

Hospitality

Simply stated, this gift involves opening your home to others. Serving a meal and making them feel welcome. Some of the most effective Christians I know exercise this gift well. They may not have some of the flashier gifts, but they make a difference for Christ. A closely related gift is graciousness. There are many Christians who are the soul of graciousness, and I am thrilled to know them. When I'm with these gifted people, immediately I feel at home, relaxed, and appreciated.

Discernment

A gift of discernment is a stewardship. It is not always pleasant, but it is a responsibility.This is the gift that so many of us as businessmen have. I think of it as dedicated judgment. Too often, when we come to church, we leave our best brains at home, voting for or agreeing to things that make little sense. We don't feel the same dedication to utilize our best judgment in our Christian work as we do in our business.

(I'm not saying we should make the same judgments—I'm convinced that a church cannot be run like a business)—at least in some of its main functions. But it certainly doesn't have to be run like a poor business. Often I'm called on to make very difficult judgments in a Christian context. I find an added responsibility in spiritual matters. Those with this gift have the responsibility to speak the truth, even when it hurts.

THE STEWARDSHIP OF MONEY

You knew I would get to it—I promised you in the beginning. Hopefully I'll do it briefly and pointedly, with great conviction. I rarely talk about money, and I stay out of fund-raising because I think it could interfere with my counseling the wealthy. (They wouldn't feel free to talk to me about the intimacy of their lives if they thought I would ask them for money.) Of course I understand the importance of raising funds.

If you've been given a talent for making money—and I believe it is a talent—and it has come within the opportunity, meaning right place and right time, then you are to use it as a trust.

One of the criticisms I have of some Christian organizations is that they are sometimes dishonest with people about money, particularly with those people who have a lot of it. I have had several wealthy friends who became Christians in middle life. Immediately they were asked to serve on committee after committee and on boards of one kind or another, invited for their "prayers and counsel." The men hadn't been Christians long enough to have much of a prayer life, and they certainly didn't have any objective counsel because they didn't know anything about the operation. I have seen two or three go through some very trying times when they realized they had been taken in by over-zealous Christian leaders who really just wanted large donations.

It strikes me that those who refer to being "blessed" with money would be much better off to say "entrusted." Those who talk about being blessed give me the feeling that they think God has chosen the right person, and He couldn't have made a better decision. And I think it's an affront to the poor Christians to imply that God blesses people with money who are not deeply spiritual. We know from experience that it is very difficult for rich people to be spiritual—it is certainly possible, and we know many examples, but it is also against natural tendency. The present economic downturn is helping many Dallas Christians unlearn the prosperity theology that has been so damaging.

Our giving should be a developed reflex. Giving should be one of our good habits, not an occasional decision. When I worked for six dollars a week, six days a week, I gave sixty cents. Before I retired, my giving was into six figures, and it was not as hard to give that amount as it was the sixty cents. I'm convinced, however, that if I had not given the sixty cents, I wouldn't have given the larger amounts.

Most of what I know about giving I can put into four points:

1.   *I never enjoyed giving until I started giving more than the tithe (10 percent).*

Recently I have been involved with a dear friend who suffers from a drinking problem. He spent $50,000 in one clinic. He is a man of substance and international reputation. I have read the material he has accumulated on the subject of alcoholism. I was intrigued that studies have found that those who reach abstinence can go for twenty years and then go back to drinking. But those who have reached the joy of sobriety rarely ever go back. Similarly, those who strain to give a tithe never really enjoy it. Those who give out of love thoroughly enjoy it and are not worried about whether it's the tithe, net or gross, or how much more.

2. *Giving is the only drain plug I know for our greed.*

If we want to drain the greed out of our souls, we can do it by giving. Since I came from the poor, I know both sides of the coin. I have found that the sin of the poor is envy, and the sin of the rich is greed. I am sure the poor want me to take a kick at the rich, but let me tell you: If you have to choose between greed and envy, always take greed, because greed can bring money and envy can bring ulcers. For productive reasons alone, greed is better than envy. But greed should not be found in Christians, and giving is the way to drain greed out of the soul.

3. *Money is temporary.*

Maxey Jarman expressed the Christian's realization of the temporariness of money when, after he had given millions of dollars to Christian causes, he hit a period of financial difficulty. I asked him if he ever thought about the millions he had given away. He replied, "Of course I have. But do you realize that I never lost a dime of what I gave away—I only lost what I kept." A lot of people are waiting to give money who ought to be giving it right now.

4.   *Lack of giving is lack of love.*

I doubt that any girl would marry a man who quizzed her on how much of his money it was going to cost him to live with her. One of the evidences of love is spontaneous, often extravagant, giving. Those who have difficulty giving freely and cheerfully will find the problem is most likely weak love, not weak finances. We give because He gave.

I believe many men can make money without God's help, but I am sure it takes real prompting of the Spirit to help make the tough decisions to give it once it's made.

> *One of the evidences of love is spontaneous, often extravagant, giving.*

I would like every new Christian to have the genuine joy of giving. For that reason I want, as an old man in the faith and Christian experience, to give you a few words of warning.

Be careful of isolated verses used out of context to prove you can bribe God or get His special favor through giving to particular causes. There are millions of poor Christians who even in their poverty have tithed for years without prosperity. God isn't obligated to pay off in dollars.

Stay in contact with older, mature Christians who can keep you from foolish schemes. For example, a friend of means became a Christian and talked with me about developing a prefabricated church building that could be erected on any prominent corner in three weeks. He believed that this project, along with an appropriate sign, "Worship Here in Three Weeks," was a way to help bring in the kingdom. I assured him that the lack of church space was not the real problem. He dropped the idea. Revolutionary ideas by new Christians usually need to be monitored. Enthusiasm is great, but so is common sense.

Personally, I believe that God is more interested in our maturity, ("conformed to the image of His Son" (Rom. 8:29)) than in our money or our success. Your calendar and your checkbook write your biography. What we spend time and money on is where our treasure is: "For where your treasure is, there your heart will be also" (Matt. 6:21).

Sometimes we try to substitute service for giving or substitute giving for service. Neither can be done successfully. Both are required for Christian maturity.

Christian stewardship is much more than money but it includes money. As my friend Rev. Steve Brown says, "Now you think about that."

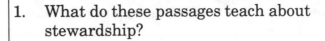

■ GROWTH STRATEGIES ■

1. What do these passages teach about
    stewardship?

    Mark 12:41-44

    Luke 19:1-27

    John 9:4

    Romans 12:2

    James 4:14

2. What is a biblical understanding of
    stewardship? What does this mean?

3. Who are people you can talk to for more
    help and information on this subject? Who
    are other resource people?

4. What do you find difficult or challenging
    about each of these?

    A. stewardship of your identity

    B. stewardship of relations

    C. stewardship of talents/gifts

    D. stewardship of money

    Which needs your most urgent attention?

5. Why is stewardship so important? What makes it difficult for you?

6. To be a good steward, what should be your next step?